CONCERNING

SPIRITUAL

GIFTS

Philip Reed

To my wife, Miranda
You are my Love and my light
I pray I can be the husband you deserve

For more information, or to book an event, contact :
(Philip@theheartofgodbooks.com)
http://www.TheHeartofGodbooks.com

Cover design by Krystin E. Moore

ISBN - Paperback: 979-8-218-22625-1
First Edition: July 2023

C O N T E N T S

Introduction

"Now concerning spiritual gifts, brethren, I do not want you to be ignorant: You know that you were Gentiles, carried away to these dumb idols, however you were led. Therefore I make known to you that no one speaking by the Spirit of God calls Jesus accursed, and no one can say that Jesus is Lord except by the Holy Spirit. There are diversities of gifts, but the same Spirit. There are differences of ministries, but the same Lord. And there are diversities of activities, but it is the same God who works all in all. But the manifestation of the Spirit is given to each one for the profit of all: for to one is given the word of wisdom through the Spirit, to another the word of knowledge through the same Spirit, to another faith by the same Spirit, to another gifts of healings by the same Spirit, to another the working of miracles, to another prophecy, to another discerning of spirits, to another different kinds of tongues, to another the interpretation of tongues. But one

and the same Spirit works all these things, distributing to each one individually as He wills."

1 Corinthians 12:1-11

In this passage of Scripture, we are given a list of the gifts of the Spirit to the church. There are ministries in the church, commonly referred to as the offices, and there are gifts of the Spirit. We will address both in this book though the focal point is the gifts of the Spirit, as mentioned here.

It will benefit you to know where I lean concerning such things. There are extreme views on these gifts from both sides. On the one side, you have what is known as the "Word of Faith" movement. This refers to those who believe we can manifest all things by decreeing and declaring them. They teach that "decreeing and declaring" is a type of prayer. This is not true. There are eleven types of prayer mentioned in the Bible; however, decreeing and declaring are not listed with them. A decree is something a king does; God decrees, but we do not have the authority to make decrees. Declaring is to proclaim, and we are to proclaim the gospel (Mark 16:15). We can prophesy as the Spirit leads, but a prophecy is when we speak forth what the Spirit of God has spoken to us. We do not prophesy at our will or our discretion.

Among this group, you will find those who take Scripture and either misunderstand it or twist its meaning to affirm their teaching. They will quote, "speaking the things that are not as though they were" (Romans 4:17). They leave out the first part that tells us that God does this, not us. They claim we have all authority and can do anything in His name, manifesting things by speaking them forth.

In Matthew 10:1, we are informed that Jesus gave authority to His disciples to cast out unclean spirits and to heal the sick. He later commands them to do such things, "heal the sick, cleanse the lepers, raise the dead and cast out devils; freely you have received, freely give" (verse 5-8). The authority given is to do the will of God. The problem comes when we exercise authority that we do not have, an unauthorized authority. What is this? When we speak forth things on behalf of God that contradict His will. We can exercise this authority over sickness, disease, and unclean spirits, but our authority doesn't match that of Jesus. I don't command Jesus. I do not have this power; it comes from God. And if I believe I can exercise power greater than someone else, I am prideful and now in danger of tapping into a power not of God. This new age teaching has been fused with Scripture, which is so ungodly. Your source should be the Scripture. If you don't understand what the Scripture may mean, you study. But you don't develop your theology by mixing Scripture with the new age movement.

A recent example of self-prophecy was during the Covid pandemic. Many well-known ministers prayed against Covid, declaring it illegal and commanding it to cease. But in Matthew 24, Jesus tells us there will be "pestilence," a word that means plagues or disease. This is a sign of the end times and is part of God's judgment. So when we rebuke something in the name of Jesus that He said would come and comes as a sign, we step outside of God's will. We will see no results when we do this.

> *"Most assuredly, I say to you, he who believes in Me, the works that I do he will do also; and greater* works *than these he will do, because I go to My Father. "And whatever you ask in My*

name, that I will do, that the Father
may be glorified in the Son. "If you ask
anything in My name, I will do it."

John 14:12-14

We can work these gifts in His name. As a part of being in covenant with God, we are given the power of attorney to use Jesus' name. That's why we pray in His name. This means we can do His work as ambassadors for Him. Prayer is a conversation between God and us, but even when we have a covenant right to discuss a thing with God (Abraham discussing the destruction of Sodom and Gomorrah), we still do not demand; we ask. We make our requests known to God by prayer and supplication, entreating, or giving an urgent request (Philippians 4:6-7).

Conversely, you have a group of people who believe we have no right to operate in any of this. They believe that the gifts of the Spirit are no longer in effect today. They teach that anyone who believes and practices such things are false prophets. It is among this group that you'll find people inclined to mock such things, thinking that it's all heresy. To this, I give a caution, the Pharisees did such a thing, and Christ rebuked them. After Jesus delivered a man from a spirit of infirmity, He was accused of working by the power of Satan. He replied, "How can Satan cast out Satan?" (Matthew 12:27). He then goes on to teach on blaspheming of the Holy Spirit and essentially equates it to this sin. It is a dangerous thing to mock the work of God. It is unwise to give credit to Satan for that which was done by the power of God.

Dr. Michael Brown says it this way: sticking strictly to the Bible, if you were to lock yourself in a closet, studying and memorizing it, when you leave that closet, you would believe that the gifts of the Spirit are still for today. The arguments against the gifts' relevance today are based on external teachings and sources (my paraphrase).

I am centered somewhere in the middle. I believe that what we are taught in 1 Corinthians 12 is, in fact, for the church, still in operation, and we all have access to it. I have done work for God through many of these gifts. But I do not align with those who believe anything we say and do can and will happen. Some teach, "Name it and claim it, blab it and grab it, confess it, possess it." I do not believe that God is at my beck and call.

On the contrary, I am at His. As He speaks to me His will, I am able and willing to do it. We are the body of Christ and are ambassadors for Him. He is the head and holds the authority; we are the body and act on His authority. We do his work on the earth as He wills. I don't command Him; He commands me. These gifts should not be feared or avoided because some have misused them. Nor should they be dismissed.

> *"Therefore, brethren, desire earnestly to prophesy, and do not forbid to speak with tongues."*
>
> *1 Corinthians 14:39*

The gifts of the Spirit are supernatural gifts given to the church by the Holy Spirit. These gifts are given to the church for its benefit, though they are not intended for the church exclusively. These are a means for the church to minister inside and outside the church walls.

My journey in understanding these gifts started in 2006. I was interning at a church in Renton, Washington. This was considered a mega-church, and to be honest, I thought it was huge! There were roughly

2,000 people who regularly attended every Sunday. I grew up in a town a little over three hours from here, and at that time, the city had about 2,400 people.

I remember one day, we, as interns, were allotted one hour with the senior pastor to ask him questions about ministry and glean whatever information we could from him. I remember asking him only one question, "Since we are a Pentecostal church and we believe that the gifts of the Spirit are for today, then why do we never teach on them? Why do we never practice them?" His answer I will never forget is, "Because we don't want to scare new believers away."

That didn't settle well with me. In 1 Corinthians 14:22, we see that speaking in tongues (diverse languages) is a sign *for* the unbeliever. I spent the next three years seeking the answer. I went to every pastor, elder, and deacon. Every teacher, student of Scripture, and anyone who had been in the church longer than a nat could spit. No one could answer my questions.

It took me the better part of 5 years before I found the answer I was seeking. And I have since continued.

In 2011, I was in a church service, and the Lord gave me the title for this book, "Concerning Spiritual Gifts," as well as three others. This was a charge to teach what I had learned. I knew I was to write, but for the next several years, I never felt it was time to write them. Until 2018, when a minister and his wife (a couple neither I nor my wife had ever met) gave us a word from God, it was time to write.

Anyone who knows what was happening at that time knows that we were under a lot of stress in our health, finances, work, etc. So being the wise man I was (I'm being facetious), I decided that God missed the timing, and it would have to be postponed. That was a huge mistake. I have learned that when God gives you instruction, He won't skip to part two until you have fulfilled part one. So as long as I sat on that command, as long as I didn't do with the word of God what He instructed me to do, He was silent. And I was miserable... until now!

Every day that goes by while writing this book, despite any stress (and there is still a lot), I am overwhelmed with the joy of the Holy Spirit! I found the key to living a life of joy, walking in obedience.

It is important to note that even though many today have a proverbial "bad taste in their mouth" concerning the gifts of the Spirit, they are biblical. And only a fool would dismiss them simply because of anything they have heard, seen, or experienced outside of Scripture. Yes, some people misuse gifts. This is what we call "sensationalism" (def: the use of exciting or shocking stories or language at the expense of accuracy to provoke public interest or excitement). This is a terrible and unbiblical practice. However, it is no reason to excuse oneself from studying them.

The gifts of the Spirit are just that, gifts freely given *to* the church *for* the benefit of the church. They are a means to draw people into Jesus. Think of it, why did crowds always surround Jesus? Because He healed the sick, cast out devils, and raised the dead! That kind of life attracts attention; the anointing is attractive. Jesus said we can do these very works (John 14:12-14). Upon leaving, Jesus sent the Spirit to empower the church with these very gifts; this empowering is commonly known as the baptism of the Holy Spirit.

The apostles taught them, the church believed and practiced them, and they haven't expired yet! At one point, the church became comfortable; it became lazy. God doesn't anoint the lazy He anoints those who do the will of the Father (Matthew 7:21).

I am writing this book to address this very topic. It must be understood that the book of Acts is the gateway from the gospels to the church. Christ came and

7

ministered in the gospels, and the Holy Spirit came and empowered the church in Acts. Everything that comes after is taught *by* those and *for* those who the Holy Spirit empowered. This isn't to say that you must have had the Pentecostal experience, as seen in Acts, to enjoy the Christian life, but think of what you miss out on by not walking in this power.

My prayer for all who read this book is that you would allow God to speak to you, revealing His Spirit to you in a new way. Don't read this with a critical heart and dismiss it. Study it, challenge what I teach but read this knowing that God gave us this blessing and wants us to enjoy it to its fullest! So before you go further, pray this prayer:

Lord, give me a heart willing to hear from you, give me a mind to understand what you say, and help me to receive revelation. Do not let any past experiences or stories I've heard prevent me from walking in the Spirit. Help me discern your heart in this study.
Amen! Amen!

CHAPTER 1

THE PROPHETS OF OLD

The promise we see in Joel 2 is that God will pour out His Spirit upon all flesh. However, there are many examples of God's Spirit coming upon and anointing men in the Old Testament:

- Moses - Numbers 11:17-25
- The Seventy Elders of Israel - Numbers 11:25
- Balaam- Numbers 24:2
- Othniel - Judges 3:10
- Gideon - Judges 6:34
- Jephthah - Judges 11:29
- Samson - Judges 14:6, 19; 15:14
- Saul - 1 Samuel 10:6,10; 11:6; 19:23
- David - 1 Samuel 16:13
- Saul's Messenger - 1 Samuel 19:20
- Elisha - 2 Kings 2:9-13
- Amasai- 1 Chronicles 12:18
- Azariah - 2 Chronicles 15:1
- Zechariah - 2 Chronicles 14:2

- The Messiah / Christ - Isaiah 11:2; 42:1; 61:1; Matthew 3:16; Luke 4:18

Through these men, we see the works and wonders of God being performed. God came upon a very select few in the Old Testament. This was to establish order (1 Corinthians 14:33). When we look at the book of Exodus and the instruction God gave to Moses for the building of the Tabernacle and its furniture, as well as the work the priests were doing, it was a picture of Heaven (Exodus 25:40). So the high priest was a symbol of Christ as the true High Priest of Heaven. God anointed one man at a time to lead His people. Once Christ came and became the great High Priest, we saw a shift in that. No longer is Israel the only nation to receive the gift of God's grace.

> *"He came to His own, and His own did not receive Him. But as many as received Him, to them He gave the right to become children of God, to those who believe in His name: who were born, not of blood, nor of the will of the flesh, nor of the will of man, but of God."*
>
> *John 1:11-13*

When Jesus was ministering on earth, He said the following: '"...all these things and greater things shall you do in My name because I go to the Father" (John 14:12). Firstly, we must understand that this is not a command to Israel alone, it's for the gentiles as well. Second, this message of the grace of God and the blood of Christ is now to be taken around the world. One man can no longer do that. And lastly, when Jesus went to

Heaven, He sent the Holy Spirit to all. And the Spirit of God has gifts that He may manifest through us.

How is this greater than the work of Christ? There are two ways this can be interpreted, greater in quality - better miracles or greater in quantity. One "work" that Jesus did was to forgive sins (Matthew 9:1-8). We cannot forgive sins; only God can (Mark 2:7). So when Jesus says we can do "these works," He isn't saying we can do everything He does. He is particular in what He commissions us to do. Jesus ministered in one place at a time. But upon the giving of the Spirit of God, all are now anointed to minister to all people. It's not to say we are greater than Christ and can do bigger and better works, but to say that our reach will be far beyond the limited area where Jesus resided. This aligns with the Great Commission in Matthew 28:18-19

> *"And Jesus came and spake unto them, 'all power is given unto Me in Heaven and in earth, go ye therefore and make disciples of all nations, baptizing them in the name of the Father and the Son and the Holy Ghost: teaching them to observe all things whatsoever I have commanded you: and lo, I am with you always, even unto the end of the world, amen."*

This command is not to pastors and elders; it is to all people. There is no requirement of credentials with a church to make disciples; God calls and anoints men for His work. If you are a child of God, you have a biblical obligation to preach the gospel. You must be the example. As it has been said many times, you may be the only example of Jesus some people see.

The Prophet Joel

Joel was a prophet, one of the select few that God spoke to concerning future things. Prophecy is one of the greatest gifts given to men by God. It is proof that God exists, second only to the resurrection of Jesus Christ. Christianity contains more detailed prophecies than any other religion. It's dangerous to include prophecy because when they don't come to pass, the entire religion crumbles. There are many religions in the world, and as one who has sought confirmation of his own, prophecy is the primary proof that our Christian faith is not in vain. No other "prophet" in any other religious faith can accurately give future prophecies as we see in Scripture.

Forty authors wrote the Bible over about 1,500 years. God spoke to these authors in many ways, often through a man who He anointed a Prophet. He told the prophets what would happen years and generations beforehand; the fulfillment is evidence that God does exist, that He is outside of time, and that He does know the future.

About every 100 years throughout Scripture, there was a prophetic voice, sometimes more than one simultaneously, such as Malachi and Haggai. After Malachi, there was a 400-year gap called the inter-testamental period, known as a period of silence; God did not speak during this period. Here are some interesting things to consider about biblical prophecy:

- 1/3 of the Old Testament prophesies are yet to be fulfilled.
- 2/3 of all Scriptures are prophetic and given through a type, symbol, or direct statement.

There are a set of rules that have been put in place to help us recognize an accurate prophetic word as opposed to a presumptuous prediction. Here are the requirements for something to be considered genuinely prophetic:

1. The prophecy must be made known prior to its fulfillment.
2. The prophecy must be beyond human foresight
3. The prophecy must give details
4. A significant amount of time must have passed between the foretelling/ publication of the prophetic and the fulfillment thereof. This is to exclude the prophet or an interested party from fulfilling it.
5. There must be clear evidence of its fulfillment

So what exactly is a prophet? A prophet sees future events not of their own will but by the power of God. This can happen in several ways:

- God can tell us of things that will come to pass through a dream, vision, or a direct word,
- God sometimes shows us in picture form, in our mind's eye (this is the way I have received prophetic words most often in my own life),
- Like with the prophets of old; Ezekiel (the Valley of Dry Bones, Ezekiel 37) and John (Revelation), He can pull people out of their timeline and take them to a future event to see it unfold before them.

A prophecy, or a prophetic word, is the foretelling of future events, and, as we will see later on, it is to edify, exhort, and comfort. This is also always true for the written Word of God. Many criticize those who say, "God told me" or, "I have a word from God". We must be careful when criticizing and ensure we take the prophetic word to the Scripture. If the "word" is of God, it will align with Scripture. The danger comes when it is a word from God, and we dismiss it as either man seeking attention or satanic. We cannot give credit for the work of God to another.

Many have misused the gift of prophecy, and for that, we have egg on our faces. Many Christians do not want anything to do with a prophetic word from God for this reason. They stick strictly to the Word of God. We cannot allow the misuse of others to determine our level of faith in God. While there isn't anything wrong with strictly staying in the Scriptures, there is a level of maturity that cannot be attained by dismissing every genuine work of God. The Bible tells us how to live and be Christ-like, which applies to everyone, but it doesn't tell us who to marry. It doesn't give us instructions on how many children to have, where to work, or what house to purchase. And often, people revert to clichés, "If it's God's will, then it will work out." "When God closes a door, He opens a window." They pray, "If it's Your will, Lord, open the door." While this isn't sinful to pray this way, it can, at times, show spiritual laziness. Let God do all the work in my life, and I'll take the path of least resistance. Some people go so far as to think that if it is God's will, then there is nothing they can do to hinder it. But that's not true. What we do with the Word of God has considerable implications in our daily life. Take, for example, Exodus 20:12,

> *"Honor thy father and thy mother: that thy days may be long upon the land which the Lord God giveth thee."*

Our obedience to this law can grant long life. Or take Ecclesiastes 7:16-17,

> *"Be not overly righteous, and do not make yourself too wise. Why should you destroy yourself? Be not overly wicked neither be a fool. Why should you die before your time?" (Esv).*

It's possible to step outside of God's plan for our life because of our foolishness, and in doing so, we can lose a blessing He has for us, or worse, we can cut our life short. We must attune our ears to the daily spoken Word of God.

Understanding the Prophecy

Many people fear prophecies, specifically those found in the book of Revelation and the end-time prophetic words given in Scripture, simply because they fear what it says. Here is something that we must keep in mind: prophecy is only negative if you are on the wrong side of it. God only punishes those who are in rebellion against He and His Word. So long as we are in covenant with Him, then His word is only to prepare us and guide us, never to harm us. As we see in Jeremiah 29:11:

> *"For I know the thoughts I think toward you, saith the Lord, thoughts of peace, and not of evil, to give you an expected end."*

But when you back up to the beginning of Jeremiah 29, God tells them many difficult years are ahead. Sometimes God's plan for your life will make you uncomfortable; in this case, the difficulties came due to Israel's disobedience to God's Word. There are many examples in the Old Testament where God warned of something terrible to come.

> *"But if you will not harken unto Me, and will not do all these commands... then I will walk contrary to you and will punish you yet seven times for your sins. I will bring a sword upon you...."*

> *Leviticus 26:14,24-25.*

Have you ever looked at unsaved people living disgustingly sinful lives and wondered why God allows that? Where is the punishment for their sin? Is He a just God by allowing that to continue? Well, as we see in 2 Peter 3:9:

> *'the Lord is not slack concerning His promise, as some count slackness, but is long suffering toward us, not willing that any should perish but that all should come to repentance.'*

Yet when a believer falls into sin, which most consider minor, God brings a swift and harsh punishment. God is patient with the sinner because of His mercy and willingness to save them. As for the child of God, we have entered into a covenant with Him. A covenant consists of terms and conditions. We see them in Deuteronomy 28, if we obey Him and His commands, He will bless us, but if we do not obey Him, He will bring the curse upon us. The curse, by the way, means a lack of His favor. A hedge of thorns instead of a hedge of protection (Hosea 2:6; Job 1:10). "For whom the Lord loves He chastens...." Hebrews 12:6.

The punishment to Israel that we see in Jeremiah is due to disobedience to God concerning the commandments in the Torah (the books of Moses or the first five books of the Scripture). Israel did not obey these commands. Specifically, they didn't follow the command to allow the land to rest every seventh year. The punishment of God was bound to come; it was now just a matter of when and through what means.

In Isaiah 39, we see that Isaiah lets in the ambassadors for Babylon, and he shows them all of the treasures of Israel (we must keep in mind that Israel was one of the wealthiest people groups on the earth at the time. Upon leaving Egypt, they took gold, silver, and jewels from the Egyptians, Exodus 12:35-36. According to author Ivan Tait, the money the Hebrews took was enough to reimburse them for the 400 years of slavery plus interest. They left Egypt with 75%-80% of the known world's wealth. Naturally, upon seeing the wealth of the Hebrews, the Babylonians decided they were the next war target). The Babylonians were how God was going to punish Israel for their disobedience. This was how God was going to assure the rest of the land.

This prophetic word came before the judgment thereof. God gave His people ample time to repent and do right, but they refused. Continuing in the way of sin, God, held by His word, was required to bring judgment. The entirety of Isaiah 39 took place 180 years before the Babylonian Captivity. Jeremiah came along 20 years before the captivity and gave another prophetic warning. Yet they continued in this sin. Prophecy serves two purposes:

1. To warn of God's impending judgment and encourage repentance to avoid said judgment

2. A sign of God's sovereignty. He is the true God; He knows the future and reveals it to us so that we may know He is God.

It is essential to judge the prophetic word effectively. How do we know it's from God? How do we know it's not just human hope or presumption? God gives us clear instructions in the Old Testament. In Deuteronomy 18:20-22 God tells us how to deal with a prophetic word:

> *"But a prophet, which shall presume to speak a word in My name, which I have not commanded him to speak, or that shall speak in the name of other gods, even that prophet shall die. And if thou say in thine heart, 'how shall we know the word which the Lord hath not spoken?' When a prophet speaks in the name of the Lord, if the thing follow not, nor come to pass, that is the thing which the Lord hath not spoken, but the prophet has spoken it presumptuously: thou shalt not be afraid of him."*

In addition to turning to the Scripture, which is the best answer, the most obvious way to judge a prophecy is to wait to see if it comes to pass! Only God is outside of time. He alone can see all things past, present, and future. Unfortunately, many people today like to put a percentage of accuracy to their prophetic words. God is 100% right 100% of the time. Sadly, many so-called prophets are not "prophets of God" but "profits of money." I can't tell you how many so-called men of God offer a prophetic word so long as you donate a specific amount of money.

If the prophetic Word is from God, it will always be right. God *is* before time, God *is* present in all places in time now, and God *is* after time. This is why Christ says, "I Am the Alpha and Omega, the First and the Last."

Imagine time as a pencil. We, as created beings, are on the pencil (the timeline) stuck in a linear path. Always moving forward, never back, never frozen. As humans, we are only able to see the present. We can plan for the future and remember/study the past, but that is where our limited point of vision extends. From your perspective -as the one holding the pencil- you can see the whole timeline. The beginning, middle, and end. That is God's relation to time. He sees the beginning, middle, and end simultaneously. He can interact with any part of the timeline as He pleases. So naturally, if He desires to reveal the end of time to someone at its beginning, He may do so.

You can see now that prophecy isn't a presumption. It isn't making an educated guess at future events. It is God, Who is outside of time, seeing the end and revealing it to us. There is no chance, only fact. Is it possible then for us, after seeing what God reveals, to change what He has shown us?

> *"For the promises of God in Him are Yes, and in Him Amen, to the glory of God through us."*
>
> *2 Corinthians 1:20*

First, we must understand that God's promises are to bring Him glory, not us. Second, they are "in Him, yes and amen." If I do not remain in Him, I will not see them come to pass. God will not promise you success in all you do and allow you to become a mass murderer. You must remain in His plan for your life. As we see in

Deuteronomy 28, God's promises are to those who enter a covenant with Him and remain in that covenant.

When you receive a promise from God, you can take it to the bank. The spoken word of God is just as valid as the fulfillment thereof. From our limited view, it hasn't happened, and doubt comes so quickly to us. But from where God sits, it's already done! The promise He gives comes from His foreknowledge of future events. He won't break His promise. He can't.

> *"God is not a man that He should lie, nor a son of man that He should repent (change His mind) Has He said and will He not do? Or has He spoken and will He not make it Good?"*
>
> *Numbers 23:19*

God cannot change His mind. That is called regression. That does not mean that the promise we receive from Him will always be fulfilled, however, because the promises He gives are conditional, the condition being that we remain in Him (see also all of John 15).

Throughout this book, we will be focused on the work of God in our daily lives through the gifts of the Spirit.

CHAPTER 2

HEARING GOD

Does God still speak today? Many say and believe that He does not. To that, I ask, why did God stop talking? From creation until the church's birth, God has spoken to His people. Not always audibly, spectacularly, or in some massive display of power. So, for what reason did God stop talking? And when exactly did He stop? God does still speak. Now, a lot of people use the compiling of the Bible as proof that He no longer does. They say, "We have the completed written Word, and there is nothing else God has to say."

In the Old Testament, God spoke selectively to certain people, as we have already established. They would, in turn, relay that message to the children of God. But a change has happened since then, on the day of Pentecost. God used to come upon select individuals; now, He has offered His Spirit to all people.

We will be getting in-depth on the different gifts of the Spirit, but it's important to note that 3 of the gifts of the Spirit fall into a category we call the "gifts of revelation." In these, you have a *word* of wisdom, a *word* of knowledge, and the discernment of spirits. This word is from God, and it is through the Holy Spirit that God speaks to us today. How did Peter know that Ananias and Sapphira had lied? He didn't have spies watching them. The Holy Spirit gave him a *word* of knowledge about this thing. In Greek, the word is "logos," which generally refers to a written word, not "Rhema," meaning a proceeding word. But logos can be used about a spoken word as one of the definitions is "a word uttered by a living voice." "Uttered" means "spoken." Peter didn't go to the Scriptures and find a passage telling him this was a lie. The Holy Spirit revealed this to Peter in his spirit with a word of knowledge.

I wonder how people pray to God about decisions when they don't believe God can or chooses not to answer them. Is prayer not a conversation? Although God spoke only to certain people concerning the prophetic in the Old Testament, He did speak to all kinds of people. He walked with Adam and Eve every day. He talked to Cain and Able, both of whom were not called a prophet. Enoch, Hagar, Jacob, Job, the list goes on. They heard Him because they listened. They weren't all prophets. And that is an important distinction; you are not a prophet simply because God speaks to you. If you are hearing God, it means you understand prayer. So why is it that we reduce prayer to us telling God our desires and then expecting Him to do something for us, presenting us with desirable opportunities? The fact is, no relationship can truly grow without communication. In 1 Thessalonians 5:17, we read;

"Pray without ceasing."

This doesn't mean constantly staying on our knees and talking with God. We must have scheduled time in prayer with God, but we must also learn to keep an open line of communication with God, like when driving in a car with someone sitting next to you. You don't always sit there leaning in, looking at them, and waiting for them to say something, but you are listening for when they do. You are aware of their presence even

22

when they aren't directly talking or interacting with you. We must learn to cultivate this kind of relationship with God. When we do, and we start to hear from God, we can know his heart in the specific situations in our life.

> *"My sheep hear My voice, and I know*
> *them, and they follow Me."*
>
> *John 10:27*

The recipe for this is found in the fear of the Lord. The fear of the Lord is to recognize God for Who He is and worship Him because of it. When we become aware of God's presence ever with us, it starts to change the way we live and interact with people. If Jesus physically manifested Himself by your side all day, how would that change your life? Would it affect the things you say? Where you go? Once we understand that God is always with us, it becomes easier for us to develop a lifestyle pleasing to Him. When we live a life pleasing to God, we can better recognize His voice.

He Will Speak

In the gospel of John, Jesus is talking to His disciples. And He is telling them that He will return to the Father in Heaven, and when He goes, He will send His Spirit. Look at what he says in John 16:13-14

> *"However, when He, the Spirit of truth,*
> *has come, He will guide you into all*
> *truth; for He will not speak on His own*
> authority, *but whatever He hears He*
> *will speak; and He will tell you things*
> *to come." He will glorify Me, for He will*
> *take of what is Mine and declare* it *to*
> *you."*

23

The Spirit of God, Who hears what Jesus says, will relay that message to us. This is a proceeding Word that the Spirit relays. What the Spirit says will never contradict the Bible, but He still speaks today.

We not only can but should hear the voice of God! In my own life, when I have received a word from God, it's when I ask him what is on his heart. By doing this, I become aware of His presence and attentive to His voice. We are so self-consumed that prayer in our life often looks as though He is our genie and we are the master of the lamp. We ask Him for His favor and protection without offering our time and obedience. This is an immature life. We want the Spirit of God to bless us but not to challenge us. We often see this in the Pentecostal circle; it's called sensationalism, seeking the gift and neglecting the giver. The gifts are, in turn, not used for God's glory but for attention. "Seek God; He wants to give you stuff." It seems that too often, the church body is seeking the manifestation of God through gifts, through how He can give us stuff. As Steve Sampson has said, "Seek His face, not His hand; it's almost as if He knows what we need anyway." When we put our friendship with God first, our needs are met.

The Giver is Greater than the Gift

> "This is how you can recognize the Spirit of God, anyone who acknowledges that Jesus Christ has come in the flesh is from God, but every spirit that does not recognize Jesus is not from God."
>
> 1 John 4:2

If we are in communion with the Spirit of God, we will not be deceived because God exposes everything that is not of Him and illuminates everything

24

that is of God. If you want to hear God and more clearly recognize His voice, you must spend more time in the Word and Prayer.

We need to stop making the gifts of the Holy Spirit about the gifts themselves. They are a manifestation of God. We should "eagerly desire spiritual gifts" (1 Corinthians 14:1), yes, but understand that they are a byproduct of a relationship with God.

God wants to talk to us daily. He desires to carry on a conversation with us. Seek His face, hear His voice and your life will flourish. The prophets in the Scripture learned to yield themselves to God's heart. They would spend hours on their knees saying nothing, just waiting, knowing God would speak.

Prayer is the key to the prophetic. It's a two-way conversation; we forget half of it. There are eleven types of prayer mentioned in Scripture, a twelfth one is always present but never mentioned by name. It's the most important type of prayer and the most often overlooked: listening prayer. No prophet ever received a word from God without first waiting and listening. Listening prayer is a part of every prayer though we often neglect it. But we can enter into a time of prayer without saying anything, and that's the best prayer.

Discerning God's Voice

> *"For the word of God is living and powerful, and sharper than any two-edged sword, piercing even to the division of soul and spirit, and of joints and marrow, and is a discerner of the thoughts and intents of the heart."*
>
> *Hebrews 4:12*

There is a specific structure that we must adhere to when seeking God's will in the daily spoken word. It starts with the written Word; then, we receive wisdom followed by the voice. This structure is vital! Many are misled because they think, "Well, God is speaking to me directly, so I have no need to read the Bible." Please do not do that. You are to test the voice of God next to the Word. If you do not know the Word of God, how can you know that you are hearing the voice of God?

> *"Now the Spirit expressly says that in later times some will depart from the faith by devoting themselves to deceitful spirits and teachings of demons."*
>
> *1 Timothy 4:1*
>
> *"Beloved, do not believe every spirit, but test the spirits to see whether they are from God, for many false prophets have gone out into the world."*
>
> *1 John 4:1*

Let us look at the Word. God will not speak to you through signs and wonders if you don't read His Word. It's straightforward, the will of God is the Word of God. If you are unsure whether you are in His will, read His Word. Too often, people want to go to ministries because they can receive a prophetic Word from this man of God. They chase the gifts and not the Giver. If you cannot discipline yourself enough to read the Bible, then you are not mature enough to know what to do with a prophetic word, so build a strong foundation in the Word.

Second, as we read the Word, God will give us wisdom. This wisdom is how the Holy Spirit speaks to us. He reminds us of what has been said in the Bible, and He reveals what God is speaking to us currently (John 14:26). Wisdom is the ability to apply the knowledge we have correctly, and that knowledge comes from the Word of God. You cannot use knowledge without first obtaining it. So you can see already there is a building block, first the Word, then the wisdom.

Third, God speaks to us in a whisper. Now it should be clear that a whisper cannot be heard in the noise. To hear God in the whisper, we must remove the physical and mental distractions. Our minds tend to wander; that's normal.

In the 1990s, there was a study done that showed that the average attention span of an adult was 12 minutes. The reason was that people were subconsciously programmed to find distractions due to commercials. They would watch t.v. and on average, every 12 minutes, there was a commercial. Now, with so many distractions and social media platforms designed for 60 seconds of entertainment, we must push beyond our natural inclination to do something else. I have read that the average attention span now is 2.7 minutes. And that sounds pretty reasonable. With 60-second reels, you need to catch someone's attention within the first 5-7 seconds for people to continue to watch what you have made.

I say this to let you know it is a challenge to push beyond distractions and hear God. The whisper comes in times of prayer. When I have a scheduled time of prayer, I move all distractions away and spend a significant amount of time waiting on God. It's in those moments that God speaks clearest. We can learn to hear Him throughout the day, but He desires us to get alone and wait upon Him.

Have you ever gone through a "Where's Waldo" book? He is on every page, but we must look for him to find Him. It is the same with God. He is everywhere, constantly surrounding us and working through the circumstances with us in our life. But if we do not look for Him, we will miss Him every time.

A Still Small Voice
Elijah, the prophet, struggled with this in his walk with God. In 1 Kings 19, he is running from Jezebel in fear for his life. God speaks to Elijah and instructs him to go to a mountain, the same mountain Moses was at when he asked to see the glory of God (Exodus 33:18-21). God passed by Elijah, and a strong wind followed, destroying rocks, but God wasn't in the wind. Next, an earthquake, but God wasn't in the earthquake. Then, a fire, still God wasn't in the fire—lastly, a still small voice. God doesn't speak in the distractions. He speaks in the stillness.

Keep in mind, though, not every thought you think is your own. Look at Jesus; after Peter said he would not allow Him to be crucified, Christ Jesus said, "Get thee behind me, Satan." Jesus wasn't calling Peter Satan. He understood that Peter allowed Satan into his mind and heart to tempt him to sin in this way (Matthew 16:23).

Another example is found in Acts 5 with Ananias and Sapphira; after lying about the land they had sold, Peter said, "Ananias, why has Satan filled your heart to lie to the Holy Spirit...?" He gave over to the temptation of Satan and planned this in his heart.

With every thought we think, we can always trace our thoughts to the root of it. We can think back and understand what made us think about certain things. Maybe you heard a song or smelled a familiar smell that brought back a memory. But when thoughts come into our heads, and we have no reasonable explanation for how we started to think about it, it wasn't our thought. Amos 4:13 says

> *"For behold, He Who forms mountains, and creates the wind,* Who declares to man what His thought is, *and makes the morning darkness, Who treads the high places of the earth - the Lord God of Hosts is His Name!".*

How do we differentiate between God's voice and our own intrusive thoughts? Mike Winger explained it with lucid dreaming. When you are dreaming, and you are questioning whether or not it is a dream, it is most definitely a dream. You never question reality when you are awake, you only question it when you aren't awake. It's the same with hearing God; if you are unsure it's Him, then it is probably safe to say it isn't Him (Mike Winger, 2023, my paraphrase).

Some thoughts come from Satan, and some from God. It's relieving to know that God will not judge us for our thoughts. We will give an account of every "idle word" (Matthew 12:36), and we will be judged (Revelation 20:2; Romans 2:6) and rewarded (Revelation 22:12) by every deed. (Note: I am in no way saying that salvation comes by works, God has made it very clear that it is solely by the blood of Jesus, but we are rewarded for what we do for the kingdom of Heaven).

> *"For out of the abundance of the heart, the mouth speaks."*
>
> *Matthew 12:34*

So the best way to stay pure in deed is to be pure in your heart. Paul instructs us on how to do this in Philippians 2:5, "let this mind be in you which was also in Christ Jesus." Though we aren't judged by our thoughts, we will find our words and deeds are fueled by those thoughts. As the saying goes, "Garbage in, garbage out."

I work at a company where a large portion of the people speak Spanish. Some of them I work pretty close with, and they don't speak English, and since I don't speak Spanish, we are learning to speak each other's language. What I have come to understand is that it is impossible to be fluent in a language until you learn to think in that language. The same applies to our walk with God. So to live Christlike, we must think Christlike. By thinking Christlike, we are open to hearing from Him daily and moment by moment.

God wants to speak to you every day! And while there are examples of people in Scripture asking for a sign from God (Gideon), and it wasn't sinful to do so, we can miss out on a conversation with God by doing this. I believe it is vital for spiritual growth to seek God's voice in our life for today.

In Matthew 4, when Satan tempted Jesus, He replied, "Man shall not live by bread alone but by every word (rhema) that proceeds from the mouth of God." "Rhema," the proceeding Word. If it's proceeding, then He hasn't stopped.

When God speaks to you today, you can treat His Word as true as the written Word. The spoken prophetic word of God is just as accurate today as it is the day it comes forth. If He spoke it, it will happen. And with that, you will find battles. When God tells you you will have a child you've been wanting for years and unable to conceive, you will have that child. But as soon as the promise comes, so too will the doubt. That's why we can and should use the prophetic Word of God to war. In the same way, Jesus used the Word of God to rebuke Satan. Like Paul instructed Timothy;

"This charge i entrust to you, Timothy, my child, in accordance to the prophecies previously made about you, that by them you may wage a good warfare"

1 Timothy 1:18

This book will be written and published. As well as four others. I'm confident in that because God has instructed me to write the books He gave me, and it's been confirmed by others who didn't even know me. There is doubt that comes my way, especially on the financial front, but God promised He would see to it that I have all I need to finish this task, and I will!

Another way God speaks to us is through His peace;

"And the peace of God which surpasses understanding, will guard your hearts and minds through Christ Jesus."

Philippians 4:7

"For He Himself (Jesus) is our peace...."

Ephesians 2:14

"God is not the author of confusion but of peace."

1 Corinthians 14:3.

Peace is associated with the character of God more than 20 times in the New Testament. Sometimes when faced with a decision, He will guide you by giving peace with one of them.

"There is no peace," says the LORD,
"for the wicked."

Isaiah 48:22

Keep in mind that there is a difference between peace and pleasure. It's easy to confuse the two at times. One of the beatitudes is to be a "peacemaker." Notice it isn't a "peacekeeper." Keeping peace is easy; you just keep your mouth shut. Making peace is the challenge; there is confrontation with it. So be wary not to confuse the two. And just because there is no opposition doesn't automatically qualify it as the Lord's will. God will often call you to do things that make you uncomfortable. Peace is internal and exists even amid chaos. (For more on hearing God in our lives today, check out the book, "You Can Hear the Voice of God" by Steve Sampson)

CHAPTER 3

THE RUWACH HA KODESH

As we study through the Scripture on the gifts of the Spirit, we need to understand who the Spirit of God is. We know that God has a Spirit, as seen in Genesis 1:2

> "...and the Spirit of God was hovering over the face of the deep (surface of the water)."

God has a Spirit, but His Spirit isn't separate from Him. God exists in three persons, the Father, the Son, and the Holy Spirit. You'll notice in the great commission Jesus didn't refer to them separately but as a single unit, a whole. This has been a topic of confusion for some time. Even the Israelites had trouble understanding this:

> "Hear O Israel: the Lord our God, the Lord is one! You shall love the Lord your God with all your heart, with all your soul, with all your strength" Deuteronomy 6:4-5

The word used here for God is: "Elohyim," meaning: "These are God". "These" is plural, and "God" is singular.

Israel had just come out of Egyptian bondage here. The Egyptians worshipped over 400 gods, so naturally, hearing the name "Elohyim" would bring confusion, as if to say He is just another god. So God coupled His name with the word "one" (echad), meaning: a union, a quantity, or an ordinal number one (Genesis 2:24). Echad would be used when speaking of a cluster of grapes.

What He is saying here is that He exists as three distinct persons yet is only one God. There have been many metaphors to try to help us understand this.

One means to teach this is to say that God is like water. He is a liquid, a solid, and a gas. He isn't three different things; He exists in three different forms. The problem is that some teach that God takes on different forms. In the beginning, God was the Father who created all. Later God took on the state of flesh and became Jesus. Then when Jesus ascended to Heaven, He took on the form of the Spirit, which those who teach this say He isn't the Spirit of God but the Spirit of Jesus. Except we see, for example, at Jesus' baptism that God the Father spoke, God the Spirit descended as a dove, and God the Son (Jesus) was being baptized. If God just took on different forms, then how do we explain this event?

A second method is to say that God is like an egg. There is the shell, the white, and the yolk. Again, the problem with this is that it suggests there are "parts" or "divisions" to God. Three different beings work in unity. But He isn't three Gods. There is one God; there is "echad."

It's easiest to understand it this way; the human being. You, as a human, consist of a body, a spirit, and a soul. Yet you are just one you. I am just one me. There are three distinct parts that all have a specific job. However, if any one of those parts were removed, then we would cease to exist. But we aren't three people, just one.

As we move to the New Testament, we see the name Holy Spirit, but this "Holy Spirit" doesn't appear in the Old Testament. What we see is the Spirit of God. So are they different?

> *"Then the temple of the Lord was filled with the cloud, and the priests could not perform their services because of the cloud, for the glory of the Lord filled the temple".*
>
> *2 Chronicles 5:13-14 (also see 2 Chronicles 7:2-3).*

When everything in the temple was in order - the furniture, the activity of the people, and the priests - then God would manifest Himself among the people. Since no one could see His face and live (Exodus 33), He would manifest Himself in the cloud or the "shekinah" - a name which in Hebrew means "the visible manifestation of God."

On the day of Atonement, the high priest would enter the tabernacle (portable tent) to offer up the sacrifice to atone for all of the sins of the people of Israel for the year. He would light the sacrifice on fire and burn it.

This was about a 30-minute process; during this time, the people would remain silent (check out Revelation 8:1). This silence was because they were on the proverbial edge of their seats. They were waiting to see if God would pardon them for their past sin and grant them favor for the coming year. If there was ever a time to be nervous, it was now.

He would offer the sacrifice on the altar and light it on fire. While this was happening, he would speak to God in a language that no one understood. It was only spoken on this day by the high priest during the time of the sacrifice.

Since everyone was quiet outside the Tabernacle at this time, they could hear him speak. This prayer language came to be known among the Hebrew people as "the language of God." This was something that only the high priest could speak on this day in the Holy of Holies. It was a priestly blessing.

There were many supernatural things taking place at this time. But one I find most intriguing is the wind. The Tabernacle covering was made of goat skin - when it rains, the goat skins tighten and prevent any water from getting through. A wind would blow through the Tabernacle, creating a distinct sound. When it would rush through, the goat skin would expand, and you would hear the wind. Then the wind would stop, and the skins would retract. This made the curtain of the Tabernacle look like lungs filling up with air, while the sound of wind rushed by, then deflating. The Tabernacle was made up of three parts:

1. The Outer Court
2. The Inner Court (Holy Place)
3. The Holy of Holies.

The wind moving the curtains of the Holy Place was described as the "Ruwach ha Kodesh," which translates to "the wind of the holies."

The word "ruwach" can be translated as "breath," "wind," or "spirit" (it is the same word in Genesis when we are told God breathed the "breath" or "spirit" of life into Adam). Thus, it can be rendered "the Spirit of the Holies" or the "Holy Spirit." The name "Holy Spirit" is a description of who He is.

It is also important to note that the Holy Spirit is never referred to in Scripture as "it." He is always referred to as "He," a masculine being. God the Father is a He. God the Son is a He. God, the Holy Spirit, is a He.

He is known as a wind, as seen here. But also a fire, as we will see in Acts 2. And He is represented in the Tabernacle as the Menorah. When you read how the menorah should be built, in our English Bibles, it says "it" in reference to the menorah, but in Hebrew, it says "His." Because the Holy Spirit is symbolized here.

The Baptism of the Holy Spirit

> "When the day of Pentecost came, they were all together in one place. Suddenly the sound like the blowing of a violent wind came from Heaven and filled the whole house where they were sitting. They saw what seemed to be tongues of fire that separated and came to rest on each of them. All of them where filled with the Holy Spirit (Ruwach Ha Kodesh) and began to speak in other tongues as the Spirit enabled them".
>
> Acts 2:1-4

Peter addresses the bewildered crowd and makes the connection between the prophecy spoken of by Joel (2:28-31) and this event. The start of the Joel prophecy is here.

I also want to point out that these men here who received this outpouring had already received the Holy Spirit, as seen in John 20:22:

> *"And when He had said this, He
> breathed on* them, *and said to them,
> 'Receive the Holy Spirit.'"*

What they received in John was the indwelling of the Holy Spirit. It's what we call salvation. The Spirit of God fills you when you confess Christ as your Lord and Savior. But in Acts 1:8, we are told that the Spirit of God came upon them. Jesus set the example for us, He did no miracles until He Himself received the Holy Spirit. We too, are to wait for the same Spirit of God to come upon us. This is what we call "the baptism of the Holy Spirit." So what's the difference between the indwelling of the Holy Spirit and the baptism? When you confess Christ as your Lord and Savior, the Spirit of God moves into you.

> *"Or do you not know that your body is
> the temple of the Holy Spirit* who is *in
> you, whom you have from God, and
> you are not your own? For you were
> bought at a price; therefore glorify
> God in your body and in your spirit,
> which are God's."*
>
> *1 Corinthians 6:19-20*
>
> *"In Him you also* trusted, *after you
> heard the word of truth, the gospel of
> your salvation; in whom also, having
> believed, you were sealed with the
> Holy Spirit of promise, who is the
> guarantee of our inheritance until the
> redemption of the purchased
> possession, to the praise of His glory."*
>
> *Ephesians 1:13-14*

Upon receiving salvation, the Spirit of God fills us and seals us. He fills us, meaning that He comes to live within us. Sealing us means He has marked us as His own, meaning we belong to God. Like they used to do when writing letters, the name of the addressee written on the front and the wax seal on the back from the owner or author of the letter. But the baptism is a little more. "When we accept salvation, we receive the Holy Spirit; when we are baptized, we release the Holy Spirit" (David Diga Hernandez, 2023)

We can look at the baptism of the Spirit the same way we look at baptism in water. It is to submerge yourself in water. It is to immerse yourself in the Spirit. This is the anointing and the empowering for the ministry. Everyone who is saved has the Holy Spirit within them, but not everyone who is saved understands how to access the Holy Spirit. They have received salvation, but they are not walking in victory. When a baby is born, they have all their senses. They have so much capability, but they must learn how to use all of it. They can talk, but they have to learn how to do it. This is the process of walking in the Spirit.

We tend to talk as Christians about growing in Spirit. Your spirit can't grow, but you can allow the Holy Spirit to have more of you. And when you do, you will find a new level of intimacy with God and new power as a believer.

CHAPTER 4

JOEL'S PROPHECY

"And it shall come to pass afterward, that I will pour out My Spirit on all flesh; and your sons and your daughters shall prophesy, your old men shall dream dreams, your young men shall see visions: And also upon the servants and upon the handmaids in those days I will pour out My Spirit."

Joel 2:28-29

There are several important things that we need to acknowledge. First, this is for all people, not just the apostles. And the promise is not for the generation of the apostle exclusively. In Acts 2:39, Peter says this is "for as many as are afar off." It is a multigenerational promise! This phrase, "all flesh," does not limit anyone. Included in this are both Jews and Gentiles alike.

Next, the sons and daughters here show us that it isn't just for men or women alone but for people of all ages. It is important to note that there is no age limit on who can receive this outpouring. Though there are different functions, we can all accept this gift.

We also see the servants. He is speaking to one who owns servants, and God says that His outpouring is not limited to the masters and free but also to those who are servants. He gave gifts to all!

What are the Last Days?
Let us look at Scripture concerning the last days. In 1 John 2:18, we read:

> *"Little children, it is the last hour; and as you have heard the antichrist is coming, even now, many antichrists have come, by which we know it is the last hour".*

Jesus gives us some extensive teachings accompanied by signs of the end of the age (referenced here is the "church age"). But let's look at this prophecy and see what it tells us.

After the crucifixion of Jesus Christ and His resurrection three days later, Jesus spent 40 days on earth continuing to minister. Before ascending to Heaven, He gave His disciples this command

> *"And behold, I am sending the promise of My Father, upon you. But stay in the city until you are clothed with power from in high"*
>
> *Luke 24:49*

They waited, watching and praying, and on the day of Pentecost, we read

> *"...they were all with one accord and in one place. And suddenly there came a*

sound from Heaven, as a rushing mighty wind, and it filled the whole house where they were sitting. Then there appeared to them divided tongues as of fire, and one sat upon each of them, and they were filled with the Holy Spirit and began to speak in other tongues as the Spirit gave them utterance".

Acts 2:1-4

Do you see anything familiar? A cloud, wind, fire, and tongues (other languages), just like we saw in the Old Testament during the Day of Atonement. Everything God gave to the High Priest of old, He has given to every one of us. After all, He has made us be a kingdom of priests (1 Peter 2:9). He is our High Priest; we are a kingdom of priests.

Once all had seen and heard, Peter stood up to address the crowd. Everyone heard what everyone was saying in their tongue, even though those speaking it didn't know their language. Peter explains that what is happening here is what Joel prophesied about, "...the last days...."

Now onto the expiration date of this prophecy:

"...and I will show wonders in the heavens and in the earth, blood and fire and pillars of smoke. The sun shall be turned into darkness and the moon into blood, before the coming of the great and awesome day of the Lord".

Joel 2:30-31

What is important to note is that with every prophetic word given in Scripture, you will also see the fulfillment of said prophecy. Peter tells us that what happened on Pentecost was the beginning of the last days. How much more are we in the last days now? We can see when these gifts will cease elsewhere in Scripture. Let's look ahead at 1 Corinthians 13:8-10

> *"Love never fails. But where there are prophesies, they will fail; where there are tongues, they will cease; where there is knowledge, it will vanish away. For we know in part and we prophesy in part, but when that which is perfect has come, that which is in part will be done away with".*

One can argue that the Word of God is the perfect thing spoken of by Joel. And though the Word of God is perfect, infallible, and inerrant, it is not what is being referred to here. The Scripture is the written Word of God, and Jesus is the Living Word of God. That which is perfect refers to Jesus and His return. We can further see this by looking at the rest of this passage in Joel. He tells us of the coming "...blood, fire and pillars of smoke...".

Blood and fire can allude to bloodshed; pillars of smoke may concern volcanic eruptions and possibly nuclear fallout or chemical gases. What gives this away is the last part:

> *"...the sun shall be turned dark and the moon to blood...".*

Where in Scripture do we see this happening? Revelation 6:12-14. During the tribulation period. This event will occur after the release of the four horsemen upon the earth, followed by the establishment of the seven-year peace treaty. We aren't there yet. In

Hebrews 11:1, we find another thing to keep in mind concerning the ceasing of the gifts

"Faith is the substance of things hoped for, the evidence of things unseen."

Who is our faith in? Christ! In Heaven, we will be with Him and see Him. There will be no need for faith. Look at the rest of the gifts:

- Tongues (diverse languages)
- The interpretation of tongues
- Prophecy
- Healings
- Working of miracles
- A word of wisdom
- A word of knowledge
- Discerning of spirits

Which of those gifts will we require in Heaven? We will have one language (Zephaniah 3:9), we will not die (Revelation 21:5), we will not get sick (Isaiah 33:24), and the list goes on. There is no need at that point. These gifts will cease when we arrive in Heaven because they are here only to minister to us and for us in this fallen world. Our relationship with the Spirit of God, and the Godhead as a whole, will completely transition upon our arrival in Heaven. In our resurrected bodies we will become fit for a sacred space.

The many who believe that the gifts of the Spirit have ceased and are no longer for today will not experience them. You must believe in a thing to experience it. You will not find salvation if you do not see your need for it. Dare I say; if you deny the rapture, you'll be left here. It is the same with the gifts of the Spirit. God will not impose His gifts upon anyone who denies that they are still in operation today.

So might I give a caution, don't deny the gifts without first seeking God's instruction on them? Don't take someone else's word for it. Look it up and study it through prayer and the Word. It's a terrible thing to go through your Christian walk, not realizing that you never accessed something so wonderful and free!

The Historical Ceasing of the Gifts

> "Be glad then, you children of Zion, and rejoice in the Lord your God; for He hath given the former rain faithfully, and He will cause the rain to come down for you - the former rain, and the latter rain in the first month."

> Joel 2:23

> "Therefore, be patient brethren, until the coming of the Lord. See how the farmer waits for the precious fruit of the earth, waiting patiently for it until it receives the early and the latter rain."

> James 5:7

Rain is a picture of the Holy Spirit outpouring (Hosea 6:3; Zechariah 10:1). The colliding of the early and the latter rain is the outpouring of the Holy Spirit.

We have seen the early rain in the book of Acts and how the church grew to fruition because of it. There is, however, a so-called "dry spell" when referring to these gifts. It is because of this that many today believe that the gifts of the Spirit have ceased. This belief is called, appropriately enough, cessation or cessationism. Let's take a look historically to get a better understanding of what happened during this time.

In the fourth century, A. D. the church stopped speaking in tongues. Many believe that the Spirit of God left. He didn't; the church stopped seeking Him.

Many people and churches love the Lord, but they do not know the history of the Holy Spirit outpouring. We know that the outpouring of the Holy Spirit, accompanied by the gifts of the Spirit, happened in the first century, according to the book of Acts. The gift of speaking in tongues happened until the fourth century. We know this as the testimony of early church fathers (pre-Nicean) tells us in their writings that they all cast out devils, healed the sick, and spoke in diverse tongues. So the outpouring of the Holy Spirit continued long after the apostles. This evidence opposes a church doctrine that the gifts died out with the apostle's death. We also know, historically, that the gifts began to slow in the fifth century for several reasons:

1. Christianity was legalized,
2. Priests were honored,
3. The church as a whole was honored and,
4. Buildings were constructed for the church members to worship together publicly

Everything shifted from faith to a more relaxed religion. This is precisely what we see in many churches today; they have become comfortable in their faith and ultimately lazy! God doesn't anoint the lazy! When we go through Scripture, we are told that God calls people, leads people, and anoints people, but He never uses people. When we use things, we dispose of them when we are done with them. God is not done with us! God was not done with the church when they became lax in their faith and testimony. But He does not call and anoint the lazy! As a free nation, we should be sharing our faith all the more! We have the legal right to preach the gospel, so what stops us? The empowerment of the Holy Spirit? Our lack of urgency? Most likely, our comfortable lifestyle. It's easy to be a "one day a week Christian."

This serves as proof that without the persecution of the church, the church body becomes lazy in its faith. The church didn't need to rely on the Spirit of God for guidance in wisdom and knowledge or healings and miracles because they were now a respected part of the community. This is true even to this day. Because the church was no longer persecuted, it stopped seeking the empowerment of the Holy Spirit. The gifts of the Spirit didn't die or cease; the church no longer wanted them.

This led to the condition of the church for the next eleven centuries, from the fifth to the sixteenth (the Dark Ages). The church became comfortable. It was during this time that the Roman Catholic Church was formed.

In 1517, Martin Luther - while doing penitence going up the stairs on his knees - heard God speak to him, "The just shall live by faith" (Hebrews 10:38). He then proceeded to write his 95-page thesis and nailed it to the door of the church. This began the Reformation, where the Protestant church was formed. This movement continued, and in the 1800s, there was a renewal of the Holy Spirit movement.

Martin Luther printed a Bible in the common tongue, and the Catholic Church was outraged. They claimed that the commoner couldn't read it. They wouldn't understand what was being said. They taught that only a priest can understand the Word of God. A former pastor of mine grew up Catholic and shared that, although everyone in the Catholic Church had a Bible, they were not to read it. This was done with much reason as the Catholic Church started doing many practices that were not biblical or were founded in the

Old Testament, before Christ. This was the first time the common people had their bible. They had never heard of the Holy Spirit outpouring. There may be several reasons why it wasn't taught, but this movement gave a jump start to the gifts of the Spirit in the church.

I'm willing to bet that anyone who has been in a Pentecostal denomination or has studied its formation of it knows about the Azusa Street Revival. On April 6, 1906, William Seymour, an African-American preacher, led seven others in prayer. They were suddenly struck down as though hit by lightning, and they began to speak in tongues, just like the early church in Acts 2. Word got around, and people began to attend as they were curious about what had happened.

It was said that every night, William Seymour would put a wooden crate on his head before he led the church in the preaching of the Word. Sometimes he would have the box on his head for an hour or more. Though no one knows why he did this or what he was doing under the crate, many believe he was praying in tongues, waiting for God to instruct him to speak. He did this every night.

They held these services at an Azusa Street Methodist church. Many people came and were healed of all kinds of illnesses, delivered from demon possessions, etc. This revival went on til roughly 1909. Out of this revival, there were many Pentecostal churches formed.

This Azusa Street Revival has been credited as the start of the Holy Spirit outpouring in the US and is called the "latter rain." However, it began ten years prior among the Cherokee Indians. Let's look at their story.

(For more on the Azusa Street Revival, I would recommend the book, "They Told Me Their Stories" by Tommy Welchel).

The Cherokee Outpouring

I first learned about this through the ministry of Perry Stone, he has a sermon on the Cherokee outpouring, and I find it pertinent to this teaching.

It has been thought that the Cherokee Indians are descended from Israel and are Jewish people. This may seem odd at first, but when you begin to study what the Cherokees and the Jews have in common, it isn't so far-fetched. James Adair (1709-1783) was a native of Ireland who went to North America for trade. He lived among different Indian groups and wrote about their customs and culture. Here is a list of the parallels he found between the Cherokee and the Jews:

- Their division into tribes (Jesus is referred to as the "Lion of the tribe of Judah"),
- Their worship of Jehovah (Yahweh),
- Their beliefs in a theocracy,
- Their belief in the ministration of angels,
- Their language and dialects - similar to Hebrew,
- Their manner of counting time,
- Their elders, prophets, and priests,
- Their festivals, fasts, religious rites,
- Their daily sacrifice,
- Their oblations and anointing,
- Their law of uncleanness,
- Their cities of refuge,
- Their raising the seed of a deceased brother.

So much of this is strictly the Jewish means of life that one can only assume the Cherokee were, at one point, part of the Jewish nation. It doesn't stop there, however.

When they would eat meat after a hunt, they would throw the first piece in the fire almost as an offering to God, something that the Jews did every time they gave a "tithe" to God.

When beating their drum, they would chant, "hall-le-lu-yah," Hallelujah, a Hebrew word that means "to praise, lift, and exalt Yahweh."

It is also believed that they had what was called the mezuzah. This was a piece of paper with the Scripture Deuteronomy 6:4-5, encased in a metal tube and placed on the doorway of the house of the Jews. They would kiss their fingers and touch the mezuzah on their way in and out of the house. As the blessing of God said that they would be blessed coming in and blessed going out.

In 1849, the Cherokee were forced from their homeland and went on what is now known as the "Trail of Tears." They lost their land, but 47 years later, roughly 120 Cherokee gathered together when the Spirit of God fell upon them, and they began to speak in other tongues. They didn't even know what it was. God was pouring out the "latter rain" upon these people. This was in 1896, ten years before the Azusa Street Revival.

They were given their true inheritance, the first to receive the outpouring of the Holy Spirit in these last days, but they also received something else, dreams and visions.

Joel prophesied that in the last days, we would receive dreams and visions. Every Cherokee I have personally met, whether Christian or not, has dreams. Regularly. And they say they almost always come to pass.

The Day of the Lord and the Day of Christ

We finish this prophecy by looking at "the great and terrible (or awesome) day of the Lord." What is the day of the Lord? Upon researching the day of the Lord, I came across two different phrases that I had thought for the longest time were interchangeable. That's the "day of the Lord" and the "day of Christ". However, they are referring to two separate days/events. So let's look at them:

The Day of the Lord:

- Isaiah 2:12: "...For the day of the Lord of hosts shall be upon everyone that is proud and lofty, And upon everyone that is lifted up; and he shall be brought low."
- Isaiah 34:8: "...For it is the day of the Lord's vengeance, and the year of recompense for the controversy of Zion".
- Isaiah 61:2: "...To proclaim the acceptable year of the Lord, and the day of vengeance of our God; to comfort all that mourn;."
- Jeremiah 46:10: "...For this is the day of the Lord God of hosts, a day of vengeance, that he may avenge him of his adversaries: and the sword shall devour, and it shall be satiate and made drunk with their blood: for the Lord God of hosts hath a sacrifice."
- Amos 5:18-20: "...woe unto you that desire the day of the Lord! To what end is it for you? The day of the Lord is darkness and not light. As if a man did flee from a lion, and a bear met him: or went into the house, and leaned his hand on a wall, and a serpent bit him. Shall not the day of the Lord be darkness, and not light? Even very dark, and no brightness in it".

The Day of Christ:

- 1 Corinthians 1:8: "...who should also confirm you unto the end, that you may be blameless until the day of our Lord Jesus Christ".
- Philippians 2:16: "...holding forth the Word of Life , that I may rejoice in the day of Christ...".

The day of the Lord is described as a terrible day, one of darkness and judgment. The day of Christ, on the other hand, is one of rejoicing. The day of Christ is when Christ comes for His bride, the church, and takes them to be with Him in Heaven; this is referred to as the "rapture." Whereas the day of the Lord follows the day of Christ, it is when God pours out His wrath on the wickedness of man, the judgment for the wicked.

In summary, the outpouring of the Holy Spirit begins in Acts 2 and ends in the tribulation period (Joel 2:31; Revelation 6:12-14). We are living in the season of this prophecy. Everything described here is available to every believer.

CHAPTER 5

DREAMS AND VISIONS

Before we go to Paul's teaching on the nine gifts of the Spirit in 1 Corinthians 12, I want to break down the first part of Joel's prophecy: dreams and visions. These are a part of the Spiritual blessing for the last days, but when we look at what Paul teaches, he never mentions these two. It's for a good reason. When looking at the nine gifts, you may notice that aside from mentioning all nine, he doesn't give instructions on all. He only teaches on the gifts of utterance; tongues, the interpretation of tongues, and prophecy. The reason is that healings never cause controversy in the church. Neither did wisdom, discernment of spirits, etc. The only things that stirred up strife were the spoken gifts. That was, then, the focus of his teaching, which we will get into later.

I believe that the main reason dreams and visions were not mentioned is that the church already had a reasonably decent understanding of them. They both appeared in the Old and New Testaments alike.

And there were some prominent examples of them in the Old Testament.

Dreams Vs. Visions
Let us first look at the difference between dreams and visions. I have been taught while growing up in church that dreams happen when you are asleep, and visions happen when you are awake. This is based, I believe, on two of the more common Scriptures involving them. But that isn't true.

Visions in the day: Numbers 24:4

> *"The utterance of him who hears the words of God, Who sees the vision of the Almighty, Who falls down, with eyes wide open"*

Vision in the night: Job 33:14-15

> *"For God may speak in one way, or in another,* Yet man *does not perceive it. In a dream, in a vision of the night, when deep sleep falls upon men, while slumbering on their beds."*

Dream in the day: Matthew 27:19

> *"While he was sitting on the judgment seat, his wife sent to him, saying, "Have nothing to do with that just Man, for I have suffered many things today in a dream because of Him."*

Dream in the night: 1 Kings 3:5

> *"At Gibeon, the LORD appeared to Solomon in a dream by night; and God said, "Ask! What shall I give you?"*

Another recent difference I have heard is that visions are literal - what you see is what you get; there is no need for interpretation - and dreams are figurative or symbolic. Here are the problems with that teaching:

- In Daniel 8, we are told that Daniel has a vision, and it is symbolic. The angel Gabriel must tell him the meaning of it.
- In Matthew 3, Joseph has a dream, and it is very literal. No symbolism whatsoever.

God tells us what the difference is in Numbers 12:6

> *"Then He said, 'Hear now My words: If there is a prophet among you, I, the LORD, make Myself known to him in a vision; I speak to him in a dream.'"*

God reveals Himself to us in His nature in a vision; God speaks to us in a dream. It is said that dreams are the language of the Spirit of God. Now, we must remember that "no one can see His face and live." Remember, though, that Moses was asking to see God's face/glory while in the flesh. Moses could not do that. However, in Isaiah 6, we are told that Isaiah was brought into the throne room of God and saw the Lord. Moses was in the flesh and could not see, whereas Isaiah was in the spirit and could see.

> *"God is Spirit, and those who worship Him must worship in Spirit and truth."*
>
> *John 4:24*

Since God is Spirit, when He "makes Himself known," He reveals His Spirit to us—no shrouding Himself behind anything. A vision is when God pulls us out of this reality (like taking your spirit to Heaven while your body remains on earth) and takes us to His reality; He shows us the spiritual realm. We see this happen with Ezekiel when God pulled him by his hair. He took him out of where he was, his own time and place, and brought him elsewhere.

A dream, on the other hand, is when God meets us in our realm. We see things in their physical realm. He "speaks to us." God doesn't speak in ways with which we are unfamiliar. In other words, He enters our physical realm, as the Angel of the Lord did in the Old Testament.

Dreams and visions can both happen while sleeping and while awake. Likewise, they can both be literal and figurative in their interpretation.

As far as visions, I have had a few, and in each one, my senses were in overdrive. I recall in one that I could smell the Spirit of God. It was the most beautiful smell. Nothing like I can compare it to here on earth. In another, I could feel what was going on in the core of my body as I was standing in the presence of a multitude of angels in Heaven while we waited for the Lord to appear! Every cell, every drop of blood, all of it, moving throughout my body, nothing was unknown or hidden. Visions have a way of standing out. I have never doubted in my mind that I had a vision. Nor have I ever forgotten a vision. I'm more careful about sharing my visions than my dreams. I think there is a level of maturity that accompanies visions in the same way there is when hearing God.

Understanding Dreams

It isn't always easy to know what a dream means upon receiving it. It can be confusing and, at times, discouraging. Especially when we feel a sense of urgency with the dream. First, I think it helps if we know the source of the dream. There are three sources:

1. God - if He gives you a dream, it's true.
2. Satan - if he gives you a dream, it's a lie.
3. Your flesh - when your flesh dreams, you are seeing the desires of your heart.

There are two main things to do to understand your dream; first, pray. And this goes hand in hand with what we discussed in the last chapter, learning to listen and hear God. He wants to tell you about your dreams. Second, seek the answer in the Scripture.

The Jews have four levels of interpreting Scripture, and I think this is an excellent place to break that down as the interpretation of dreams follows the same pattern.

Biblical Interpretation:
1. *Peshat*: understanding the simple meaning of the text.
2. *Remez*: an allusion or an allegorical and philosophical level of study.
3. *Drash*: At the regal level, the Bible is understood in riddles and parables - Jesus taught like this often, as did all rabbis.
4. *Sod*: the hidden meaning or mystical level. Revelation is often given at this level - Matthew 13:11

Dream Interpretation:
1. *Literal*. What you see is what you get. There is no symbolism and no need to interpret. Maybe in your dream, someone gave you a message. Take it at face value.
2. *Allegorical*. Everything is symbolic of something. Usually really basic in its

interpretation. Like Peter on the day of Pentecost: "This is that which the prophet Joel spoke of...".

3. *Philosophical.* Everything you need to understand the dream is in the dream, but you have to think about it to understand. God isn't hiding anything from you, but He is making it difficult to understand so that you commit it to prayer. Like in Ezekiel chapter 1, the throne of God looks like the Tabernacle.

4. *Hidden level.* Job 33:16. God seals our dreams to keep us from pride. It's a way for Him to assure you that He knows your future. It's all in His hand.

According to the Talmud, a dream that wakes one up or occurs in the morning demands an interpretation, as does a dream that leaves one feeling sad. (The Talmud is a commentary of Jewish discussion concerning oral law as it relates to Jewish law, ethics, customs, and history. It attempts to clarify parts of the Torah that may not be clear. For this reason, the Talmud is not on the level of Scripture; we can relate to it more like a Bible commentary than a direct word from God).

Don't be discouraged if you don't understand the dream immediately. God reveals them to us in several different ways:

1. *Instantly.* God will reveal the meaning of your dreams to you upon receiving the dream when you awake.

2. *Simultaneously.* He may speak the meaning of your dream to you as you dream it.

3. *Through Writing.* He can give you an understanding of your dream as you

write it down. He did this with Daniel. Dreams are subjective. Things will make sense in a dream that won't always make sense upon waking up. Dreams - being subjective - are not straight lines. So don't think objectively while trying to interpret them. Writing them down in a circle or waves may help to think it through.

4. *Through Time.* He may unfold the meaning of your dream as you walk throughout your day. Sometimes it may be years after you dream before God shows you. This is why it is essential to keep a dream journal. You can go back to them later.

I have found it very important to keep a journal by my bed. When I wake up, I write the dream down. If you wait and go back to sleep or get up and do other things, you will forget it. And just like king Nebuchadnezzar, he had to ask if anyone could tell him what he dreamed.

I think most people have had an experience of deja vu, the feeling of having already experienced something. Science will tell you it is a lapse in your short-term memory. Half your brain registers what is happening now, while there is a delay in communication with the other half, giving you short-term amnesia. But I think it's simpler than that. God has shown us our future through the night and sealed it.

> *"For God may speak in one way, or another,* Yet man *does not perceive it. In a dream, in a vision of the night, when deep sleep falls upon men, while slumbering on their beds, then He*

opens the ears of men, and seals their instruction."

Job 33:15-18

The purpose of this is to show us that God is outside of time and that He knows what is going to happen. It's reassuring to know that such a loving God already knows everything and takes care of them before things even happen in our life.

Understanding the Symbolism

The best place to go when trying to find what something means in a dream is the Scripture. God loves symbolism, and we see it throughout the Bible. In Jewish hermeneutics (the art and science of interpretation), there are 32 laws of interpretation. One of these laws is that of "the first mention." When you wish to know what a particular symbol means, go to the earliest mention of it in Scripture. Whatever it symbolizes, there, is what it symbolizes throughout Scripture. If I mentioned a lamb, what would you think it's a picture of? Jesus, the Lamb of God, Who takes away the sin of the world. Sheep would be us, the church. A rainbow is a symbol of God's promises. What about a serpent? Satan right? Note that there are some exceptions. For example, in John 3:14-15 we read:

"And as Moses lifted up the serpent in the wilderness, even so must the Son of Man be lifted up, that whoever believes in Him should not perish but have eternal life."

Jesus is symbolized as a serpent here because "He Who knew no sin, became sin that we might become the righteousness of God" (2 Corinthians 5:21).

We can look at a dove for a more detailed symbol. The dove symbolizes the Spirit of God. We see this at the baptism of Jesus as the Spirit of God descended as a dove. A dove has nine primary feathers on each wing. Nine on the one side for the nine gifts of the Spirit, and nine on the other for the nine fruit of the Spirit. The dove has five primary feathers on its tail, symbolizing the fivefold ministry of the apostle, prophet, evangelist, pastor, and teacher.

Scripture is the first place one should go while seeking the meaning of a dream. However, that isn't the only place. There are some personal and social symbols. Most people like dogs, and dogs can represent friends. But if you have had a bad experience with a dog, you may fear them. God knows your language and speaks to you in that manner.

It is crucial to establish a two-way conversation with God. Hearing Him speak is the best way to attune your ear to His voice. It will help you better receive the interpretation when you learn to recognize His voice.

I want to share a dream I had recently that was quite significant. I was in my bedroom, and my wife wasn't there, just me and one of my two dogs, Ansel. I was standing against the back wall, and Ansel was with me to my left.

Out of nowhere, a snake appeared. It was small, maybe a foot long, and looked like a newborn snake. It started to hiss, and I saw that it was getting ready to strike, so with my back on the wall, I slid down and reached over to Ansel, grabbing his rear and trying to push him away.

As soon as I did that, the snake struck and bit deeply into flesh. For my life, I can't remember if it was me or Ansel he got. Almost as if I looked, but everything was fuzzy.

As soon as the snake's teeth sunk in, a lump appeared below his head and moved slowly down his body, like he had swallowed flesh. A few moments later, the lump turned into a second head. And when it appeared, it also struck. The same thing happened. A lump, a third head, and a third strike.

This happened until seven heads filled the snake's whole body from the top of its first natural head down to its tail. Now it was a twelve-inch-long set of snakeheads.

This was so intense that I woke up, and my whole back was arched, and the weight of my body was pressing my head into the pillows. My entire neck was super stiff, and I had pain throughout my neck for the next few days. This was a warning of the spiritual struggle that would take place over the next seven years.

Many people would say this isn't from God because I was terrified of the snake, and I even had a physical reaction to it. But I beg to differ. In Genesis 15, when God appeared to Abram, we are told that horror and great darkness fell upon him. God doesn't speak through emotions, but having an emotional response when God speaks is normal. When people encounter God or angels, they are told, "Do not fear." So we don't judge a dream or vision based on our emotions, but we must understand that emotions get involved. There will be peace if it is from God. And peace is internal, not an emotional response. Your spirit can feel peace when your body or external circumstances are in chaos.

Preparing to Dream

Statistics show how often people dream and how some dream only in black and white while others are in color. The fact is, when God wants to speak to you in a dream, He will. But there is a way to receive dreams from Him more, simply by valuing them. In the same way, God won't speak if we don't listen; God won't give us dreams if we don't appreciate them.

One good practice is to have a dream journal by your bed. Prepare to write everything God tells you. And pray before you go to sleep. Ask the Lord to speak to you. He wants to; you have to want to listen.

I recently had a dream, and I woke myself up singing. It was a song from my childhood that I had forgotten we sang in church. It was in my heart for the next few days to remind me of God's saving grace.

CHAPTER 6

MINISTRY AND SPIRITUAL GIFTS

I want to take a brief moment to look at the types of gifts mentioned in the Scripture and give a distinguishing explanation of them. In Ephesians 4:8, we read:

> *"When He (Christ) ascended on high,*
> *He lead captivity captive and He gave*
> *gifts to men."*

The word here for captive is the Greek word "etymology," and it means "to make captive, to capture or to take captive." As sinners, without the redemptive work of Christ through the shedding of His blood, we were already captives of Satan. What we see in His final work here is that Christ captured those who were in Satan's captivity. He took back what the enemy stole! In Acts 2:31, we read:

> *"... that He (Christ) was not*
> *abandoned to Hades, nor did His flesh*
> *see corruption...."*

When Christ died, He went to Paradise, a compartment under the earth that housed all the righteous saints who died before Him. The place "Paradise," also known as "Abraham's Bosom," is separated from Hades by a great chasm. In Luke 16:19-31, Jesus tells us a story of a rich man and Lazarus.

To summarize this account, there was a beggar named Lazarus who had sores and was unclean according to the Law of Moses. He desired to be fed by the rich man's crumbs that fell to the ground. They both eventually died, and angels carried Lazarus to Abraham's Bosom while the rich man was tormented in Hades. The rich man begged Abraham to let Lazarus dip his finger in the water and touch his tongue. Abraham explained that there was a chasm between the two, and they could not cross over.

We are then told that the rich man was praying that Lazarus would be allowed to go back and tell the brothers of the rich man about the reality of eternity, and, to his disappointment, he was informed that not even one being raised from the dead would be able to convince them.

This account is not a parable, by the way. A parable is a presentation of spiritual truths using earthly illustrations. How can you explain to someone something they have never seen? By relating it to things that they have seen. This story is not a parable, however. Jesus straightforwardly presents truths. Here is the proof that this is an accurate account and the two men did live:

1. Parables never name people, as we see here in verse 20, "Lazarus,"
2. This story follows the rules and teaching patterns of "pashat," a Hebraic word describing direct teaching as opposed to

"drash," symbolic teaching (see chapter 5),

3. Of Jesus' 38 parables, in all of them, He uses words such as, "the Kingdom of Heaven is like...". There is no "likening" here,

4. In parables, we see symbolism; there is no such symbolism here.

When Christ arose from the dead, He was the firstborn among many (Romans 8:29). The saints in Paradise appeared with Christ (Matthew 27:52-53). Upon Christ ascending to Heaven, He was surrounded by a cloud (Acts 1:9), and that cloud, I believe, are the saints who arose from their graves. They are called a "cloud of witnesses" in Hebrews 12:1-2. They are now in Heaven, waiting to return to earth with Christ for the millennial reign.

(Note: Paradise was a temporary holding place for the righteous saints who died before Christ's resurrection. Now we go directly into Heaven. Likewise, Hades is a temporary holding place for the sinners who have died and are currently dying. Hades will follow Death into Hell after the Great White Throne Judgement, Revelation 20:14-15).

I believe Christ is taking those held captive and releasing them to Heaven, their eternal dwelling place. I know there are many varying thoughts on this passage, and I won't get into all of them. We know that Christ took those who belong to Him with Him to Heaven.

The order of events for believers now that Christ arose is that upon our death, we are now taken immediately to Heaven to be with Him (2 Corinthians 5:8). It's interesting how so many believe that upon death, we go to a holding place called purgatory and we can pray them out of there into Heaven. Yet Jesus tells us here that, at least, some of those who died lost are actually in Hades praying that we on earth would choose to follow Christ. They cannot escape after their death. We only have our time here on earth to decide whether we will surrender to God and find redemption through the blood of Christ. If that decision isn't made before our death, there is no hope.

> *"And as it is appointed for men to die once, but after this the judgment, so Christ was offered once to bear the sins of many. To those who eagerly wait for Him, He will appear a second time, apart from sin, for salvation."*
>
> *Hebrews 9:27-28.*

Going back to Hebrews 12:1-2, we are told that He led captivity captive, and He gave gifts to men.

It wasn't until I started to attend a non-Pentecostal church that I realized a lot of people group the ministry gifts mentioned in Ephesians with the gifts of the Spirit. These two are separate, and what I can say is this, your life will change when you can recognize that and have an understanding of the gifts in 1 Corinthians 12. There is nothing quite like having access to the gifts of the Spirit all the time. Here is the list of the different gifts given to men by Christ

1. Ministry gifts - Ephesians 4:10
2. Service gifts - Roman's 12:7
3. Spiritual gifts - 1 Corinthians 12

Let's take a bit more of a detailed look into these gifts.

Ministry Gifts - Ephesians 4:10-13

> *"(He who descended is the one who also ascended far above all the*

heavens, that he might fill all things.) And he gave the apostles, the prophets, the evangelists, the shepherds and teachers, to equip the saints for the work of ministry, for building up the body of Christ, until we all attain to the unity of the faith and of the knowledge of the Son of God, to mature manhood, to the measure of the stature of the fullness of Christ."

It is often taught that this is a list of the five-fold ministry offices. However, look at how this was written; "... some to be apostles, some to be prophets, some to be evangelists and some to be pastors AND teachers". Pastor and teacher are to be the same. It is the same person who operates in the anointing of both. Now, that isn't to say you can't be a teacher and not a pastor; this means that if one is to be a pastor, he must be able to teach. Teachers are a part of the function of the church, separate from the pastor. Also, we must remember that in the great commission (Matthew 28:18-19), all are called to make disciples; preaching/teaching the gospel does that. So often, people think that preaching and pastoring are synonymous, and they aren't. A pastor must be able to teach and preach. But a teacher and preacher don't have to pastor.

The Scripture does not call any of these ministries listed here "offices." But it's a term we use in many churches. Christian jargon, if you will. Maybe "ministry branches" would be more acceptable for some? There is a reason, however, that this term is associated with this teaching here. In all of these ministries, they are full-time. For the church to properly function (I'm talking about the church as a whole, the body of Christ worldwide), these roles must be fulfilled.

Five groups are mentioned here, but I do not believe all are functioning today. Now, those who disagree will read verse 13, which tells us they will be in operation until we become unified in faith and knowledge of the Son of God. We have not obtained that yet so I understand the reason for believing they are for today. However, other passages of Scripture also talk about these ministries, and we need to keep them in mind.

If we back up to the beginning of this teaching in Ephesians 2:20-22, we see the function of both the apostle and the prophet:

> "built on the foundation of the apostles and prophets, Christ Jesus himself being the cornerstone, "in whom the whole structure, being joined together, grows into a holy temple in the Lord. In him you also are being built together into a dwelling place for God by the Spirit."

Jesus is the chief cornerstone, the Living Word of God. The apostles and prophets are the foundation, and the rest of the church builds on them. This implies that these two offices are no longer in use today. The foundation laid was the work of the New Testament Scripture. The church is founded on that work. They served their function. In Acts 1:21-22 when selecting an apostle to replace Judas, they were required to have seen the Lord Jesus after His resurrection. No one meets that requirement today. Many say that it was an isolated requirement; I beg to differ. There is no reason to assume that stance from Scripture; that is an individual interpretation.

The primary purpose of the apostles was to start the church. They were to lay the groundwork for the church, which was temporary. We do not need that now. Yes, an argument can be made that we still go to places without churches and build there. But this passage in Ephesians leads one to believe that this work was finished with the apostles of Christ. I am convinced that the apostolic ministry was not continual but phased out after the church was established. In 1 Corinthians 15:1-11 we are informed that Christ appeared to the twelve apostles, then to five hundred, then to James and the other apostles. So there were more than just the twelve. But Paul goes on to say that Christ appeared "lastly to me." Last of all, what? Apostles. This tells us that Paul was the last. And we must remember that there was a twenty-six-year gap between when he became an apostle and when he is writing this. That's a long time not to have any more apostles commissioned.

I understand that this is a topic many disagree on, and to that, I say, so long as Christ is preached, does it matter? I think we get too hung up on titles in the church. We are all called to make disciples, whether in a church setting, foreign country, or relationships with people in our sphere of influence. These titles don't matter. Let's say apostles are for today, and you fulfill that ministry; you can do so without waving around that title. The only title you and I should concern ourselves with is "a child of God." Christ's work on the cross is what matters.

With all of that being said, let us look at the offices in their respective duties. This passage in Ephesians lists these offices in descending order. First, an apostle is a church planter. Its actual definition is "one who is sent on a mission." That is the most basic definition of an apostle that exists. The church did not coin the term "apostle"; there were apostles before Christ came. So what was an apostle? Well, he would be an admiral who traveled with a group of other skilled men that would essentially colonize places. This group, under the admiral's leadership, would go to a place where people did not live, and they would build up a community and settle there. So in the church, an apostle was someone who, like Paul, traveled to a place where there was no church and, with a team under his leadership, built a church there. And you'll notice that Paul didn't travel alone; he had a team. An apostle should be able to build a church from the ground up, fulfilling the church leadership roles until he can delegate those roles to the local body of Christ.

Second is the prophet, who must be able to hear from God and speak it forth to the body of Christ. Prophets get a bad reputation nowadays. Too many have been seen on television or in mega-churches claiming that the more money you give, the better the prophetic word you will receive from God. You have direct access to God through the name of Jesus. Don't pay a man for something that God wants to give to you directly! You harm your relationship with God if you go to a man for a word. You begin to rely on others to tell you what God wants you to do instead of opening a direct line of communication with Him.

If anyone is selling prophecies, then it isn't from God. This is what Peter dealt with in Acts 8. Simon, the sorcerer, saw that the gifts of the Spirit were given through the laying on of hands and offered money for it. Peter rebuked him. The work of God is not about profit.

The prophet is still needed in the church, though. Every prophetic word you get will first be in line with Scripture; it will never be in contradiction. To hear from God, you must first go to the Word. And second, it will be a confirmation of what God has already been speaking to you about. In 2 Peter 1:21, we are told that a prophet speaks as the Spirit of God moves them. It's like a ship; without the wind, it will not move. A true prophet spends more time in the presence of God than he does before people. He was waiting for the wind of the Spirit to move.

There is a distinct difference between the office of the prophet and one who operates in the gift of prophecy. If I develop a close relationship with God, allowing Him to impress Himself upon me, which is really what prayer is about, not merely talking to God but allowing God to impress Himself upon us, then I can know the heart of God and speak it forth. It is God speaking a Word, us relaying that Word, and the Word coming to pass. All prophecy follows this structure.

Now, when we look at Scripture, I think Daniel Schott said that roughly 80% of prophecies are simply the prophet speaking forth the Word of God into a situation. What is the Word of God? It's His heart. Out of the abundance of the heart, the mouth speaks. You want to prophesy, read the Word. By knowing the Word, you learn God's heart, and by speaking it forth, it becomes prophecy.

This is why it is so essential to be of good character. It requires a life of complete dedication to God. It involves sacrifice beyond what most people are willing to give. By the way, God does require more from some of us than others (Matthew 25:14-30). The anointing of the prophet requires your entire life to be in line with God. There is no room for a pet sin. If a prophet lacks the character and discipline that a man of God must have, he will cease to prophesy. Why, you may ask? Because he no longer knows the heart of God.

Fruit, over the content you speak, is more important in your life as a prophet. Because people can get the truth from a bad source and speak said truth with ill intent. We are told that Satan is the father of lies, yet we wrongly assume he can only tell lies. He is skilled at taking the truth, giving us enough to believe it, and then twisting it to lead us astray.

Though a prophet speaks forth future events, we would be in error to assume that that was all a prophet did. The prominent role of a prophet was to make the Word of God known. How many times do we see prophets give a warning of impending judgment? When this word came forth, they preached "repent."

Many prophets in the Old Testament were seen with other prophets learning under them. Samuel, Elijah, and even Elisha had someone under his ministry. They were not being taught how to speak forth their desires. On the contrary, they were to speak forth God's heart. A prophet's job is more about teaching one to hear the voice of God as opposed to constantly prophesying, though they do that as well. They are teaching these men how to live a Godly life, to be men of Godly character, and to hear God's voice.

Third is the evangelist, who can share the gospel with the lost—usually traveling outside of the reach of the local church. Their goal is to preach the good news of the gospel, Jesus Christ. They often operate in churches with an outreach ministry, focusing on bringing in people from outside the church.

Lastly, we have the role of the pastor/teacher. This is what we have in our local churches. These offices are how the church operates. They are vital for the function of the church. The pastor is the shepherd. They are to have the vision of where God is taking the church and what He is doing in the church body and through them.

The church body cannot grow beyond where the church leadership is willing to go. The pulpit drives the church. James talks about a bit placed in a horse's mouth will give you control over its whole body. The mouthpiece or the head provides direction for the entire church. If the pastor doesn't preach or teach about the gifts of the Spirit, then the church will not see them in operation. This is why it is vital to be intentional about what you seek in a church. If a church is stuck with a group of people who gossip all the time, and the leadership will not address it, it will poison the whole church body.

This is the function of church leadership! To hear from God and relay that word to the body of Christ! By doing so, it ensures unity in the local community. God may move in a certain way in one part of your town and in a different way in another. The way the Lord is ministering in New York is different than the way He ministers in Evansville, Indiana. So we must find a church whose leadership is in line with the Spirit of God to minister to the lives of the local community effectively.

Gifts of Service/Aiding - Romans 12:4-8

> *"For as we have many members in one body, but all the members do not have the same function, so we,* being *many, are one body in Christ, and individually members of one another. Having then gifts differing according to the grace that is given to us,* let us use them: *if prophecy,* let us prophesy *in proportion to our faith; or ministry,* let us use it *in our ministering; he who teaches, in teaching; he who exhorts, in exhortation; he who gives, with liberality; he who leads, with diligence; he who shows mercy, with cheerfulness."*

This is a list of gifts for the church body to function. I say the body because the offices we just looked at are for the leadership to shepherd and guide the body. Under their authority, the body should operate.

Again, the church body cannot grow beyond its leadership. What we receive in the church from the ministers should be a direct word from God. The pastor gets the word from God and gives the word to us. The body receives the word from the pastor, and we give it to the world. Our job in the community is simple; we get the Word, we give the Word!

This doesn't mean the individual cannot receive a word from God, as we will soon see. The pastor is the church's leader, drawing the believers in the community into one mind and goal. It is a means to hold each other accountable and to be mutually encouraged in our faith, but also to find unity.

> "And as you go, preach, saying, 'The kingdom of heaven is at hand.' "Heal the sick, cleanse the lepers, raise the dead, cast out demons. Freely you have received, freely give."
>
> Matthew 10:7-8.

Many think that this means ministries shouldn't charge for the material they produce. Not so! There are ministry expenses, and they need to be covered. When a pastor writes a book and a worship leader records a song, these expenses must be covered. That is why God required a giving of tithe to pay for the ministry. But to those outside of the church umbrella, they have to raise money in other ways. Offerings are above and beyond the tithe meant to further the ministry of Christ.

Let me then ask, what have we freely been given? The message of salvation, so preach it! What have we been freely given? Healing, so heal the sick! What have we been freely given? Deliverance, so cast out devils! This is the function of the church but not its goal. The goal is to seek out the lost and lead them to Christ. The gifts given, all the gifts, are what equip us to do so.

Gifts of the Spirit - 1 Corinthians 12:7-11

> *"But the manifestation of the Spirit is given to each one for the profit of all: for to one is given the word of wisdom through the Spirit, to another the word of knowledge through the same Spirit, to another faith by the same Spirit, to another gifts of healings by the same Spirit, to another the working of miracles, to another prophecy, to another discerning of spirits, to another* different *kinds of tongues, to another the interpretation of tongues. But one and the same Spirit works all these things, distributing to each one individually as He wills."*

It is important to note that these are the gifts of the Spirit, not the gifts of man. And though Jesus sent the comforter (Holy Spirit) Who manifests these gifts through us, we do not have a say on when and where, or even how these gifts are to be used. It is by the Spirit of God. It's dangerous to the kingdom and even the individual to try to manifest the power of God on our own (we will cover this in chapter 12).

No man can heal, but the Spirit within him does. No man can prophesy, but the Spirit of God does through him. The gifts of the Spirit are called gifts of the Spirit because we don't have those gifts ourselves. I have functioned in the gift of knowledge quite often; I don't have the knowledge of God myself. I have the

Spirit of God, and He gives me knowledge. I operate in the gift of knowledge because the Spirit of God wants to administer knowledge through me.

> *"But He was wounded for our transgressions, He was bruised for our iniquities; The chastisement for our peace was upon Him, And by His stripes we are healed."*
>
> *Isaiah 53:5*

I like how David Hernandez says, "Jesus does not heal us, He is our healing. Jesus does not deliver us, He is our deliverance". We are not anointed to introduce revival but to introduce the reviver! Jesus must be the central focus of all we do. Without Him, nothing we do would ever amount to anything. All of life is meaningless without Him. Don't seek healing or prophecy or miracles; seek Jesus!

It is important to note that just as the gifts are gifts to us, they are also gifts to others. They are a means of service. Not one gift here is intended to be used for one's gain. God heals the Christian because of His covenant; God heals the sinner because of His mercy. This is a starting point for ministering to people.

In this passage of Scripture, we see that there are three categories:

1. The Gifts of Revelation
2. The Gifts of Power
3. The Gifts of Utterance

We will spend the rest of this book looking in-depth into the different gifts listed here and the function of each. However, I think a summary of the difference between the gifts is in order. The ministry gifts are for the function of the church, and the gifts of the Spirit are for the benefit of the church.

CHAPTER 7

GIFTS OF REVELATION

A Word of Knowledge

Though the gift of knowledge is mentioned four times in 1 Corinthians 12-14, there is no teaching or example given. That does not mean that we cannot understand what is meant here. Knowledge in its most simplistic form is information. You can always gain more knowledge by studying, reading books, and listening to others with information on a particular subject.

We can do a deep dive into knowledge throughout the Scripture, but it doesn't benefit us here as, like all the gifts of the Spirit, it is given by God to man concerning a specific situation. As I just mentioned, knowledge can be gained in many ways; the best way, however, is through the Spirit of God. Keeping in mind that God is outside of time, He knows past, present, and future, and God also knows the heart and mind of man (1 Corinthians 2:11). So when we receive a word of knowledge from God, it is information that we do not yet have, and information that is obtained outside of the natural means.

It's one thing for someone informed about a situation to come to me and say, "Philip, did you know (fill in the blank) is abusing his wife?" It is another thing to have God show me that situation, giving me insight without anyone telling me.

Let me give you a personal example; there was a relative of mine, years ago, who was in the hospital. She had been there for several days. I had to work, and amid my workday, the Spirit of God had shown me that it was time for her to go home. Being led by the Spirit of God, I prayed that same prayer Jesus prayed on the cross, "Into your hands Lord, we commit her spirit." Not even a minute later, I received a text that she had just passed away.

I could not have known that. We knew she was nearing the end of her life. But when God was ready to take her home, He revealed to me that now was the time, and there is no better way to go home than through prayer!

When God shows us something outside of ourselves, it isn't a means for us to gossip. One of Satan's most effective tools against the church is gossip disguised as prayer requests. People enjoy talking about others and the drama that they face, and for some reason, we find it appropriate to "share" the information for the sake of prayer. "This couple needs us to pray because they are having trouble in their marriage and may divorce." We don't need to detail someone else's life for prayer. God knows the situation, and we can pray without the details. That is one of the reasons we pray in tongues (we will get to that in detail).

We must not abuse the gifts of God, lest He stop giving them to us. With the spiritual insight I have received over the years, more often than not, God provides us with the knowledge to pray about it and not to talk about it. The only time I share knowledge like this is when God releases me to do so. And when He does, it isn't intended for me to share with everyone, only those it concerns.

God can also give us knowledge in a way that I call a "download" of information. I have that happen a lot. While writing this book, I have been given this download. He gives me more knowledge about this subject while I'm not even studying it, just writing. And sometimes, it is so much information that I almost can't even write it as fast as I get it. It's at this point that I have to turn on my voice recorder and speak it so I don't forget it.

It happened again when my wife and I needed a new car. Finances were tight, and we were going through some health issues. One day while mowing the lawn, the Lord showed me a picture in my mind's eye of the car He had planned for us. I didn't know what type of car; I just knew what it looked like. The first car lot we went to had this exact car that was sitting there. It was out of our budget, but I knew if this was the one God had for us, He would work this out. We were able to talk them down to the price we could afford.

God can also give us knowledge through a dream. My wife, not long ago, had a dream about an old teacher of hers. In the dream, she saw the teacher and his wife in their home having a very heated argument about getting separated, as it had just come out about inappropriate behavior on his part. This dream happened before they had separated and he had moved. When asked what the dream meant, I explained that God gave my wife knowledge about a situation that, at that time, no one knew about, simply because they required prayer. God called her to pray for a situation she would have never known.

God tends to give a word of knowledge to someone to establish credit. One thing we see a lot in the Pentecostal church is people operating in the gift of prophecy. It isn't wise to take everything someone says as from God without testing it. Often a word of knowledge will come before a prophetic word so that the one hearing can know they are receiving from God. If a stranger comes to me with a word from God but starts telling me stuff about my life that they have no way of knowing, I can be confident that they are hearing from God.

A Word of Wisdom

This is not wisdom. It is not a means for you to be wise in all things. Some people are naturally gifted in wisdom. All people can gain wisdom, but this is not wisdom in a general sense. This is a word of wisdom. A word of wisdom comes from God concerning specific issues. I like the definition found in Job 33:33:

> *"...hold your peace and I will teach you wisdom."*

God is speaking to Job about his situation here. He desires to teach Job wisdom. The word here in Hebrew means:

1.   Skill in war
2.   Wisdom in administration
3.   Shrewdness in regards to affairs

Skill in war. This doesn't mean becoming a great warrior. It has nothing to do with physical strength or the ability to wield a weapon. It's about strategy. I'm not one to know much about war. I'm terrible at geography, so I'll use chess as an example.

To win at chess, you must be able to outmaneuver your opponent. When looking at the board, you must consider where each piece can move, its strong and weak points. While evaluating your opponent's potential, you must determine your strategy. You must be able to calculate your opponent's most probable course of action and preemptively counter him. Outsmart him.

Jesus told us to be "wise as serpents and innocent as doves" (Matthew 10:16). Wise or cunning. He also gives us our best strategy against the enemy, "Watch and pray" (Matthew 26:4). In this context; He is talking about the ability to fall into temptation. But what are we watching? We are to watch in the spirit.

Satan is like a roaring lion, roaming around, seeking whom he may devour (1 Peter 5:8). We are to be sober and vigilant, ready to resist him when he attacks. Unlike chess, we don't always see every piece. And Satan constantly tries to devour us, tempt us to sin, and get us to fail. God, who sees all and knows the end, can and wants to give us insight into the attacks of Satan. Satan comes at us daily and seasonally. In Luke 4:13, we are told that after Satan tempted Jesus, he left Him for a season.

There was a well-known preacher who, years ago, taught that wisdom was to receive a future word from God. Though I believe he meant well, I'm afraid that's not right. Let me explain why he taught this. If I take a screwdriver and jam it into a live socket, the result could be terrible. I'll get shocked. The ability to calculate the result of a choice I make is not prophecy; it's wisdom. But this preacher took it to mean that seeing the outcome before the action was prophecy. It isn't. Wisdom is the ability to make sound judgments based on the knowledge you have. In spiritual warfare, we can't always see this. So receiving a word of wisdom from God, Who can see all, is a spiritual gift. Foreseeing future events is the very definition of prophecy. Wisdom is to be calculated in your decisions.

Allow me to give you an example: according to the Encyclopedia of Judaica and Jewish tradition,

Goliath had a sword with a gold handle encasing gemstones. It belonged to Anak, the father of the giants. Anak gave it to his firstborn, Goliath, the oldest and the leader of the remaining giants in David's day. When David killed Goliath, he kept his sword as a relic in a secret compartment in the Tabernacle. David takes this sword - a Philistine heirloom - back to the Philistines while fleeing King Saul. By doing this, he risked his life, as all the Philistines would have recognized the sword.

Muslims/Arabs - believe in what they call Jinn, i.e., Genies. We call them demons; the Bible calls them evil or unclean spirits. An Arabic tradition states that if you kill a man with a Jinn in him, the Jinn will leave the one dead and enter into the one who killed him. Or, in the words of Jesus, "When a demon leaves one house (person), he goes through desert places seeking a new home..." (Matthew 12:43). David knew this superstitious belief and therefore played upon it. By acting insane and a madman and "foaming at the mouth," the Philistines did not want to kill him and welcome this Jinn into the city. So they left him be. After all, there was nothing the Philistines could do to bring more harm to David than what he was already going through.

David applied the knowledge he had to this situation, which was wisdom.

CHAPTER 8

THE DISCERNING OF SPIRITS

The last of the gifts of revelation is the gift of discerning of spirits. This is not a gift of discernment. It is the discerning of spirits. The reason this is such an important gift is because there are different types of spirits:

1. Holy Spirit (the Spirit of God)
2. Human spirits
3. Angelic spirits
4. Evil spirits (devils)

It's hard sometimes to know what the Spirit of God is trying to tell us. How can I tell if it's God's Spirit talking to me and not my own intrusive thoughts? This all goes back to what we discussed in chapter two on hearing God. Go to Scripture! But what about a word we receive in prayer about a specific situation in our life? Not a moral or immoral issue, just guidance. This is where the discernment of spirits comes into work.

When the Spirit of God speaks to us, He will never tell us anything contrary to the Scripture. However, He tends to tell us more specific and situational things. God wants to speak to us daily, and often it isn't about the big stuff. Sometimes God wants to talk about the things that may be considered mundane. Just a few weeks ago, the Lord showed me a new car a friend just bought. I was unaware they had bought it, but I saw them driving up in it. And sure enough, they had that exact car. This revelation held no significance in my life other than God just wanted to talk to me.

Concerning the human spirit, it seeks self-satisfaction. You don't naturally want confrontation or anything that makes you uncomfortable. So when you "feel in your spirit" anything that promotes self-seeking, it isn't of God.

Then we have angelic spirits or angels. They are known as messengers of God. I don't believe some angels have the sole purpose of delivering messages; I think all angels can and do get assigned to deliver messages. Let's look at a few Scriptures concerning angels:

> *"Take heed that you do not despise one of these little ones, for I say to you that in heaven their angels always see the face of My Father who is in heaven."*
>
> *Matthew 8:10*

> *"For He shall give His angels charge over you, To keep you in all your ways. In* their *hands they shall bear you up, lest you dash your foot against a stone."*
>
> *Psalm 91:11*

This is about "he who dwells in the secret place of the Most High." Anyone who is in covenant with God and spends time with Him in Prayer and worship does have this promise.

> *"But to which of the angels has He ever said:* 'Sit at My right hand, till I make Your enemies Your footstool'*? Are they not all ministering spirits sent forth to minister for those who will inherit salvation?"*
>
> *Hebrews 1:13-14*

Scripture gives us strong evidence of guardian angels. I believe that it's possible to offend those angels. Anything that would offend God will offend an angel. Remember, they don't want attention; that got Satan kicked out of Heaven.

In 2011, I was working at a company in Kentucky as a fork truck driver. I had gone into a forty-day fast, and this was the most intense fast that I had ever done. I wasn't too sure at the start of the fast why the Lord had been leading me to it; all I knew was that He had something in store for me. Not long after starting this particular fast, the Lord led me to read the entire Bible every 30 days. So I had a pocket Bible on me. Whenever I had free time, breaks, lunch, and when I got off work, I was in the Word. I turned to the text of Scripture throughout my day.

I then decided to fast, not just from food and media; I fasted from my thoughts. It's so easy to think about stuff all the time. We plan for the future, worry about the house payment, etc. So when I found myself doing that, I would pray, "Lord, keep my thoughts upon you. Tune my ear to what You have to say to me".

By the end of my forty-day fast, I had heard twice, in an audible voice, prophetic words from God. While driving my fork truck, wearing my earplugs, I heard a loud voice to the right and just behind me. This was an angel, a messenger of God, delivering His Word to me.

Two things need to be clarified with this; one, I'm not special. It isn't that God decided to speak to me and not someone else. I'm not "holier than thou." As previously mentioned, God desires to talk to each of us daily. Also, Jesus didn't do any great miracles without first spending time in prayer and even fasting. I learned to do both when I was seeking an answer from God. Two, I'm not giving credit to anyone but God in this. It must be made clear when angels do the work of God; it is not because they want attention. They don't. The work they do is to bring glory to God. This act of self-glorification was the very reason a third of the angels got themselves kicked out of heaven in the first place, Revelation 12:9:

> *"So the great dragon was cast out, that serpent of old, called the Devil and Satan, who deceives the whole world; he was cast to the earth, and his angels were cast out with him."*

I have shared this story a few times with people, and one thing I find non-Christians saying is, "Sounds like a hallucination," or they tell me that I'm "smoking the wrong pipe." Understanding their perspective, I may agree if the evidence wasn't so convincing. Sensory hallucinations are common when people go through extreme trauma and changes in their life. So how can I be sure that it was a message from God? I already explained; they were prophetic! God told me something that would happen in the future, and it did. People can't hallucinate about the future. We can presume, we can take educated guesses, but that's what makes prophecy the number one proof of the existence of God!

I have recently researched mushrooms and psilocybin, a psychedelic drug. I'm no expert, and no, my research did not involve recreational use. In every experience I have heard or studied, not one had a prophetic hallucination. I believe they see the supernatural realm, but they never know the future. That sets the prophetic apart from any other experience known to man.

Look at Ezekiel 37, "The Valley of Dry Bones." Ezekiel was removed from his timeline, pulled into the future, set down in this valley, and saw the holocaust. Historically, no other event has happened that has even come close to that of the Holocaust. Many Jewish rabbis have testified that the holocaust fulfilled such prophecy. In this prophecy, we see:

1. Hebrews were skin and bone (vs. 1)
2. God instructed Ezekiel to "prophesy," meaning that this was a future event and had not yet happened.
3. The phrase "House of Israel" is used. He is speaking to the nation of Israel (vs. 11)
4. "Open your graves." When the survivors came out of the Holocaust, they looked like skeletons coming out of their graves—flesh and bone (vs. 12).

We can see this same event also prophesied in Psalm 102. No drug can cause such accuracy in foretelling a future event. An even greater proof is the many prophecies of Jesus' birth, life, death, and resurrection.

There are almost 65,000 cross-references in Scripture. Many of those exist in the form of prophecies.

Lastly, demonic spirits. In Acts 16, Paul was ministering, and a girl with a spirit of divination who brought her masters a lot of money was following them and said;

> *"These men are the servants of the Most High God, who proclaim to us the way of salvation."*

This is not the Spirit of God, nor is it a ministering spirit on His behalf. This is an evil spirit, one of divination. Sometimes devils can tell us the truth about God and use it to lead us astray. Though what was being said was true, the end game was to pull the crowd away from Paul and draw them to her so that she could deceive them further.

We know that devils believe God is Who He says He is (James 2:19). You may have had this happen without knowing it while reading a book or hearing someone preach; you have an uneasy feeling. Even though what is being taught comes from Scripture, something about it is off. You get a feeling in your spirit or, as some may say, in the pit of your stomach. This is a "check in your spirit" or a caution from the Spirit of God. You know it's not right, even if you don't understand why. The best we can do is go to Scripture and look into it more. But there are other ways to know; God is a God of peace and not confusion (1 Corinthians 14:33). So if what you receive is not at peace in your spirit, it's not of God.

Understanding the Demonic

As previously mentioned in chapter one, Peter was being influenced by Satan, and again with Ananias and Sapphira, they didn't come up with the plan to deceive the Spirit of God on their own. Satan spoke into their heart, and they acted upon it. These people were not possessed of spirits; they were, however, influenced by them.

Though the focus here is not whether a Christian can become demon possessed or not, I will say that I believe a Christian can have whatever they want. Scripture is clear that spirits can vex all people, Christian or otherwise.

Legion

In Mark 5:1-20, Jesus comes to the Garasenes and finds a man possessed by an impure spirit who calls himself "Legion, for we are many."

He lived among the tombs, crying day and night (disturbing the peace), cutting himself, and no one could bind him up. And he called himself "Legion." Look at the significance of the name:

In the Roman army, a unit comprised eight men. Ten units (80 men) made one century. Six centuries (480 men) made 1 cohort. Ten cohorts (4800 men) made one Legion. An army consisted of 5,280 men. So a Legion was just shy of an army. Many spirits possessed this man. It was a pagan belief that when a person died, their spirit would dwell around that body for three days. The spirit of the dead man would attract evil spirits. If anyone possessed by a spirit had died, the devils in them would look for a new place. So it wasn't an odd thing for a man who lived among the tombs to be possessed. It was uncommon, however, to be possessed by so many.

Now if you look at this same story in Matthew 8:28-34, you will notice that it states that there were two men possessed and not just one like Mark tells us. Is this a mistake?

Looking at Matthew 12:43, Jesus teaches that when an evil spirit - or *many* in this case - leaves a place, they look for a new house (person) in which to dwell. Could it be - and I'm just asking - that when Jesus commanded Legion to "come out of him," Legion immediately left the first man and went into another? At this point, Legion begged Jesus not to make him leave the area but to send him into a nearby herd of pigs (5:9). Jesus then gave permission. Legion did so, and the herd of pigs ran down the hillside and drowned in the water (In my opinion, that is the most plausible explanation).

(Note: I also want to point out something that I think is important in this narrative. There is, among the occult, a group of people who like to become what is called a "human chalice." They call up a devil to possess them so Satan may use them. Then they want to go to Christian services where people have been known to get delivered from devils, knowing what Jesus taught that seven others would return with the first, all so that they can obtain even more devils. This isn't some sci-fi movie. I know of a pastor personally in Leavenworth, Washington, who had this happen in one of his church services. They base this practice on what Jesus teaches. They believe that somehow being possessed by many spirits increases the favor of Satan in their life).

We may look at this event in Matthew and Mark and think it was harsh. First, those pigs did nothing wrong; why would Jesus allow them to be possessed by evil spirits and drown? Second, did those pigs not belong to someone? Were they not someone's livelihood? Most likely, they did and were.

It is important to note that in the area of the Garasenes, the people were a pagan community. They worshipped the pagan god Zeus. The way that they honored Zeus was by sacrificing pigs to him. The demons wanted to be worshipped, not killed. That is why they asked to go into the pigs. What they were not anticipating was that they would drown. Jesus, the Son of the Living God, will not allow His praise to be given to another. He will not play games like this; He has too much class.

The Scripture said the people in the community were confused and told the rest of the town about the man possessed and about the pigs. The town was upset and asked Jesus to leave.

Why weren't they thankful? Jesus just delivered a man who was possessed and disturbing the peace. They were angry, not at the fact that this man was free of the evil spirits and not even that those spirits were now looking for a new place to abide; they were angry because now they had no sacrifice for Zeus. They feared the wrath of Zeus would kill them all. They just saw the most incredible miracle for which one could ask. Jesus exercised His authority over devils and, ultimately, their false god. Zeus hadn't done anything like this for them. Yet, they were so involved in a religion that they were blinded from an encounter with God. In their mind, one man possessed was a small price to pay to keep peace with their false god.

Vexing Spirits

That said, let's look at some commonplace things that happen when a spirit vexes people. We can find this here in this account of Scripture and others.

1. They tend to isolate themselves,
2. They have a fascination with death (hanging around places of death),
3. They experience emotional lows, depression, suicide, etc.
4. A lot of times, they cut themselves,
5. They become creatures of the night.

Harassing spirits can provoke people to do irrational things. Vexing spirits can sway the heart. This doesn't mean that people who experience such things are possessed, though I do think that, more often than not, there is some demonic influence and vexation.

We also know that, as Christians, we are in a spiritual war. This is not, however, an excuse for sinful behavior. Too often, people like to claim a spirit of gluttony or a spirit of lust. If everything is spiritual and demonic, I don't have to take any responsibility for my actions, and discipline is unnecessary. I think, more often than not, we need discipline and not deliverance!

> *"For we do not wrestle against flesh and blood, but against principalities, against powers, against the rulers of the darkness of this age, against spiritual* hosts *of wickedness in the heavenly* places."*
>
> *Ephesians 6:12*

As we step into the will of God for our life, we will see an increase in spiritual attacks that come in many forms, health, finances, fear, etc. It is when we spread the gospel that we find a rise in demonic attacks. That is why, as the rest of the passage in Ephesians 6 tells us, we must equip ourselves with the armor of God.

Sealed by the Spirit

> *"In Him you also* trusted, *after you heard the word of truth, the gospel of your salvation; in whom also, having believed, you were sealed with the Holy Spirit of promise, Who is the guarantee of our inheritance until the redemption of the purchased possession, to the praise of His glory."*
>
> *Ephesians 1:13-14*

How does this "sealing with the Holy Spirit" work? What is the purpose?

I traveled with an evangelist years ago. At one point, we came to a television station to record a special. Afterward, the evangelist and one of the owners of the t.v. station had pulled me aside. They wanted to talk to me concerning a harassing spirit that was vexing me. I was informed that I could receive deliverance if I would allow them to "deal" with the spirit.

Now, keep in mind I am a spirit-filled believer. The Spirit of God lives within me. They had instructed me to allow the evil spirit to possess me so they could talk to him and figure out why he was harassing me. They essentially wanted to interview him while I was possessed. They would then use the knowledge they had gained to cast the spirit out and send him to hell.

I'm sad to say that although I grew up in a Pentecostal church, we never really taught much about this. And in the previous few months, I saw God working in this man's ministry. So being my naïve self, I trusted him.

They sat there trying to call the spirit and told me to "give in" and "let the spirit speak through you." It didn't work. I was filled with the Spirit of God. Every time I opened my mouth, I spoke in tongues. It is impossible to be sealed or filled with the Spirit of God and be possessed by a devil. I didn't have to know this was false teaching; the Spirit within me was dealing with the situation.

After nearly an hour, they stopped and told me I wasn't ready for deliverance and that I somehow wanted to hold on to it. No, they were trying to make a show out of me, and God wouldn't have it. They were unbiblical in their approach of deliverance.

This is why it is so essential to be filled with the Spirit. Though I had no understanding at the time as to what was going on, God was not going to allow me to be given over to Satan.

Familiar Spirits
In 1 Samuel 28:3-25, we see that the Philistines had gathered to face the Israelites for war. When Saul saw the army of the Philistines, his heart filled with terror. Scripture said that Saul inquired of the Lord, but the Lord did not answer him by dreams, urim, or prophets.

Saul then instructed his attendants to find a woman who was a medium so he could inquire of her. (Note: mediums were people who could talk to the dead, whereas necromancers would call up a spirit to possess them, and they would allow the spirit to speak through them. It is a cheap imitation of the gifts of the Spirit, where we yield to the Spirit of God and speak forth prophecies or diverse languages). Saul had previously commanded all who practiced witchcraft to be put to death based on the Law of God (Torah). So, for self-preservation, she refused. And only upon Saul swearing by the Lord that he would not have her put to death did she agree.

When she called the spirit up, Saul asked what the spirit looked like, and she described an "old man wearing a robe." Because that pretty much clears it all up, right? Saul "perceived" that it was Samuel - because surely Samuel would be the only spirit to look "old" and be "wearing a robe". He then fell prostrate. The spirit said, "Why have you disturbed me in bringing me up?"

Saul essentially says, "God has left me!"

> *"If the Lord has departed you and become your enemy, why do you consult me (a man of God)?"*

The spirit then says that because of Saul's sin, Israel and Saul's house would be delivered to the Philistines.

There are a few things to clarify about this story. Many have argued whether this was Samuel's spirit or not. The Bible calls this a "familiar" spirit (Lev. 20:27). It takes on the form of someone familiar to the person they talk to. Here is how we know the spirit isn't Samuel:

1. The Bible never says this spirit is Samuel but that Saul "*perceived*" that it was Samuel.
2. Saul inquired of the Lord, and the Lord did not answer by the only ways God spoke to His people.
3. Saul admitted that the Lord had left Him.

God had instructed all witches, mediums, and necromancers to be put to death. So if God would not speak to Saul through the ways God allowed, why would God talk to him in an unlawful manner? Now the supposed "spirit of Samuel" prophesied accurately that Saul would die that day. How did he give such an accurate prophecy? Devils don't know the future. It's pretty straightforward; God had already prophesied to Saul previously that the kingdom would be ripped from Saul. And, well, Saul inquired of a medium, which the punishment from God for that is death. The spirit knew the Word of God, and because of Saul's disobedience, he knew that he would be killed because of it. This is one of the 18 laws of the Old Testament that required death as a punishment. So Saul's death here shouldn't come as a surprise.

So the Spirit wasn't prophesying. The spirit knew the law of God and concluded that due to Saul's actions that day, God would have him put to death. Also, remember that this passage talks about the three ways Saul sought God Before going to a medium. It doesn't say these are the only ways God spoke to people. In the Old Testament, God would talk through three types of people: a priest, a prophet, or a king. Never a witch, medium, or necromancer. He would speak in the following ways;

1. Dreams
2. Visions
3. Urim and Thummim.
4. Prophets
5. The Menorah
6. Directly

Saul could not discern between the spirit of Samuel and a familiar spirit because the Lord left him. We, however, have been given the Spirit of God, who anoints us with the gift of discerning of spirits for this purpose.

We find throughout Scripture that there are many kinds of evil spirits; though not all spirits are identified in Scripture, here are the ones we do see:

1. Bondage - Romans 8:15
2. Heaviness - Isaiah 61:3
3. Tormenting Spirit - 1 John 4:18
4. Fear - 2 Timothy 1:7
5. Infirmity - Luke 13:11
6. Jealous - Numbers 5:14
7. Principalities-
   a. Prince of Persia - Daniel 10:13
   b. Prince of Greece - Daniel 10:20
   c. Abaddon / Apollyon - Revelation 9:11
   d. Death and Hades - Revelation 6:8

I want to share a bit about the lying spirits we see named in 1 Kings 22:23. At this time, Israel was divided, Judah was by themself with a king, Jehoshaphat, and Israel had their king. The king of Israel, Ahab, was ready to go to war with Syria and claim Ramoth in Gilead. He asked Jehoshaphat, king of Judah, to join him in the war, and Jehoshaphat, though vowing to stand with him, asked the king of Israel to seek a word from the Lord through a prophet. There were around four hundred prophets in Israel, all false prophets. And they all told the king that he would prosper. Jehoshaphat, a man of God, recognized that these were not true prophets of God. God wasn't speaking by more than one person; God rules by His Word, not by mob rules, which is what we see in Israel at this time. The king did not want prophets of God; he hired "yes men" to make him feel good.

So when confronted, the king said, "There is one prophet of God who is still in Israel, but I don't like him; he doesn't tell me what I want to hear" (my paraphrase). There is all the proof you need to know that these four hundred men were only there to encourage the king.

Micaiah was the true prophet, though he was instructed to "prophesy" the same word the false prophets gave. Micaiah vowed to speak what God spoke, not what man wanted. After he was brought before the king, he said what the king wanted to hear, but Ahab knew he was lying. So Micaiah exposed the plan of God in this. It was time for Ahab to die, and his death was to come by this war. This is what man saw, but the true prophet of God, Micaiah, revealed what God spoke in the heavenly realm, "who will persuade Ahab to go to war?" A spirit came forth and said, "I will become a lying spirit in the mouth of his prophets that he may go to war and fall into battle."

There are a few things we see in this story. First, this was God's plan. Second, God announced His plan to the heavenly beings. Why? Because angels and devils don't know the future.

In the same way God reveals things to us by His Spirit; He also reveals things to the angels and devils. This isn't a new revelation, either. We see God do this in the account of Job. Satan came before God in God's throne room to discuss Job. And these meetings took place over time; we can see that these meetings happened regularly (Job 1-2). Lastly, God allowed an evil spirit to give a false prophecy concerning the king so that God's plan would be fulfilled and He would be glorified. God can use the actions of evil men to see His plan come to fruition.

This does not mean that everything that goes wrong in your life is of Satan. Just because you got a flat tire doesn't mean Satan gave it to you. If he had the authority to do so, he would do it every day. Sometimes things happen.

There is a lying spirit that is active in the church today. One who comes into the church with a supposed Word of the Lord. But he only speaks what men want to hear. You may have seen it on t.v., men who claim to be speaking prophetic words from God but are only speaking what men's itching ears want to hear (2 Timothy 4:3). I know of some who have been into the new age movement and psychic readings. You'll notice that they never merely have a word for you. They ask you questions and fish around for something that hooks you. Then the reading they give you is so vague that it can fit anyone who has had anything good or bad happen to them. That isn't a prophecy; that's a probability!

I worked at a factory in Moses Lake, Washington, years ago where a coworker, a woman in her mid-forties, had a psychic reading for me. She got this regularly, though she never went into a profession of fortune telling. She asked if I had met any girl around my age who was blonde and named Sarah. After telling her I hadn't, she said it was probably a future meeting that would soon occur. Apparently, Sarah was to be my future wife.

Now, if I wasn't the wise young man I was (I'm being facetious), I would have gone to social media and looked at all my friends to see if someone fit the description. If not, I would have looked at church, work, or anywhere I found myself to find someone who met that description. It would have been easy to find the first blonde young woman named Sarah and claim; this is her! Pursuing the relationship because I was convinced she was the one for me. In reality, there are probably hundreds of young blonde women named Sarah in that town. There are never specifics with psychics.

I have noticed that whenever there is a "profit of money" in the guise of the prophet of God, they always promise good things. They are encouraging. In Scripture, when God gives a prophecy, He often gives warnings. We know His promises are conditional and not free handouts (2 Corinthians 1:20). So why do modern-day prophets always want to give "good fortunes" to people? Maybe they are psychics and not prophets? Prophets, after all, tell you what is on God's mind; psychics tell you what is on yours.

Some people are nothing shy of false prophets, and they do infiltrate the church like wolves in sheep's clothing (Matthew 7:15). They are the ones who come into the church saying, "Thus saith the Lord" when the Lord saith not. But I often think, as with all of the vocal gifts, they are good-intentioned people who either don't understand how the gifts operate and have been misguided, or they want to be used by God so much that they try to force it. Both are dangerous, but the posture of the heart is what God is judging. Discerning the Spirit of God is vital in our relationship with Him. The more time you spend with Him, the easier it gets.

Smudge Sticks and Oil

There is a practice that goes back centuries where an individual would take a bundle of herbs (differing herbs based on the desired outcome) and light the end of it. They would then put it out and use the smoke to ward off evil spirits and bad energy. They were first using the smoke to "wash their hands" and then proceeding to their face. This is to cleanse themself of any negative energy. They would then go around their house and trace the outline of their doors, windows, and entryways. This was supposed to be done regularly. After guests visit, you would perform this ritual to ward off anything negative they may have brought, as there could be residue.

We see similar means of interacting with evil spirits throughout the Scripture. Oil symbolizes the Holy Spirit and is used to anoint people and objects. When the Spirit of God anointed a king or priest, oil would be poured over their head as a sign of their anointing for the office. It's also common to anoint the sick with oil (James 5:14).

One prime example concerns the Israelites and the Angel of Death. During their exodus from Egypt, they were required to place the blood of a lamb on the doorpost of their house, and when the Angel of Death saw it, he would pass over them and spare their life. We also see the instruction for the priest on how to purify the furniture in the Tabernacle. They were to anoint the furniture seven days for it to be holy and consecrated to the Lord (Exodus 29:36-37).

Based on the instruction of Exodus 40:9, we as believers do this ourselves over our homes. It is, in a sense, a spiritual mark of God. This was a means to consecrate ourselves and our homes to God. And whenever there is demonic activity in a house or building, anointing the home with oil and praying over it is a way to evict devils and welcome God.

So do smudge sticks do the same? The result may seem the same, but the process is different. Anointing a home with oil and praying over it will evict all evil spirits. They don't have a choice and can't come back unless invited. However, any method used to "cleanse" a home not founded in Scripture may have the appearance of clearing out spirits, but the spirits are not evicted. So why do they leave? They don't! If you do anything to please an evil spirit, allowing them to remain so long as they hold their peace, they will. But do anything against them, and they will continue to torment. We must continually offer a sacrifice to devils as a means of worship for them to allow us to remain at peace in our homes. That's how the pagans worshipped the false gods of old. "Don't make them angry lest they kill us!" God, on the other hand, will evict them, and you won't have any concerns about them again.

Satan will use any means necessary to keep your attention and faith off God. Satan's goal is to keep you blind to the power and person of God. He and his angels do still work in an orderly fashion. They plan to keep you from God's love, and deception is one of his most excellent tools.

CHAPTER 9

GIFTS OF POWER

"Now faith is the substance of things hoped for, the evidence of things not seen.

Hebrews 11:1

When I first got to know a particular church outside of the Pentecostal denomination, I was informed that they were "bapti-costal," baptists that weren't quite fully Pentecostal. The reason is that they believed that healing and faith specifically were available today to all, and they were pretty charismatic. However, as we will see in this chapter, this is not the same as saving faith; it's a different level. It's not just healing that happens when we pray for it. This is the faith and healing that defies nature. I'm confident that the gift of faith here is needed for the gift of healing and the working of miracles to exist.

Let us look at the levels of faith here and see how the gift can work in our lack.

1 No faith

"But He said to them, 'Why are you so fearful? How is it that you have no faith'?".

Mark 4:40

This narrative informs us that the disciples were in a boat, Jesus was asleep, and a storm rolled in. This was a storm violent enough that the disciples feared they would die. So they woke Him and asked how He could sleep when their life was at risk. Do you still have no faith?

Jesus questions their lack of faith because of the overwhelming presence of fear. Fear and faith work the same; they are both the belief that something that has not happened will happen. Fear is the belief in the negative, and faith is the belief in the positive. Fear is the belief that your problem will conquer you. Faith is the belief that God will conquer you and, in turn, conquer your problem. We cannot exercise fear and faith simultaneously. After all, they have seen Him do; they still have no faith.

2 Weak Faith

"And not being weak in faith, he (Abraham) did not consider his own body, already dead (since he was about a hundred years old), and the deadness of Sarah's womb."

Romans 4:19

Talking about Abraham, having received a promise years prior, one that now required a miracle,

Abraham did not get weak in faith. This is so easy to do when we have been beaten down.

In my own life, my wife and I had gone through a difficult time with health, physically and emotionally; it was difficult to believe that God would pull us through. This is where it is so crucial for us to be connected to a local church, to have a community to encourage us in our struggles. "Bare one another's burdens and so fulfill the law of God" (Galatians 6:2-5).

3   Strong Faith

"He did not waver at the promise of God through unbelief, but was strengthened in faith, giving glory to God."

Romans 4:20

The Greek renders this "but was strong in faith" Abraham was strong in faith. He had no one to encourage him. No one to go to and get council. He was the father of our faith. When all of nature came against him, he remained firm, knowing God would keep His Word.

4   Great Faith

"When Jesus heard it, He marveled, and said to those who followed, 'Assuredly, I say to you, I have not found such great faith, not even in Israel!'"

Matthew 8:10

A centurion came to Jesus, his servant was paralyzed, and he asked Jesus if He would heal Him.

Jesus agreed to go and do so, but the centurion stopped Him. He understood what it was to command someone to do something, and it got done without him doing it himself. "Speak the Word, and it will be enough."

Understand something; Jesus hadn't done this before. He loved people, and He loved interacting with them. He desired to talk to people and minister to their needs. So a miracle of this magnitude (which is what this was) was unheard of. This man's faith exceeded all the others. He believed beyond what had been seen. That is great faith!

Biblical faith is not trying to believe something so strongly that you can manifest it. Prosperity preaching teaches us that if we believe enough, God must do what we ask. Faith is not wishing something into existence. It is taking what God says and believing it. It is to trust God even when it isn't visible.

So what can we learn from this? Sometimes, like the disciples, our faith may fail. When our child is fighting for their life, or we must file bankruptcy, it's hard to trust God's provision there. This is when we need the Spirit of God to step in and exercise faith through us.

Gifts of Healing

There are different types of healing that you will find we need in life. Sometimes we need spiritual healing. People in the body of Christ can hurt us in a way that our relationship with God suffers. It's tragic, but I have experienced this more than once. Betrayal is one of the deepest wounds we can feel. And when it happens in the church among fellow believers and those we count as friends, it can take a toll on our faith.

> *"And* one *will say to him, 'What are these wounds between your arms?' Then he will answer,* "Those *with*

*which I was wounded in the house of
my friends."*

Zechariah 13:6

I have decided not to take my offense and hurt
and direct it toward God. An entire church body can
turn its back on me; I will not go to hell for someone
else's sin. I will not become bitter at God for how people
treat me.

I find it interesting how betrayal can manifest in
our life. It starts with an offense. And instead of
addressing it, we internalize it. It becomes bitterness.
Bitterness is internal; betrayal is external.

So we get offended and wallow in it. If we don't
take control of it upon its initial presentation, we will
lose control over it, and it can ruin our life. It is
important to remember that with the temptation, God
provides a way of escape. Not after we have allowed it
to fester. Not when we find ourselves in the act of sin
but with it. (1 Corinthians 10:13).

The best offense is a great defense. I think one of
the greatest examples we have of resisting sin is found
in Joseph (Genesis 39). When he was working in
Potiphar's house, the wife of Potiphar came to him to
seduce him. His first and immediate response was,
"How can I do such an evil thing and sin against
God?" He didn't hesitate. He wasn't giving himself time
to reason this situation; he had decided beforehand.
And he never voiced what he desired; he spoke only of
God in the situation. We have to be prayed up before we
find ourselves in these situations.

Another example where we may find healing
may be an issue with a father, or lack thereof, that
hinders us from developing a healthy relationship with
God. That's a physical problem that can cause a spiritual
hindrance.

I have been fortunate enough to have a father in my home. My parents are still married after, well, a lot of years. I've had my issues, and there have been disagreements, but God has kept our relationship strong, and I dearly miss them as they live far away. Unfortunately, not everyone has had that kind of experience. There are too many broken homes, abuse physically, substance, and even sexual abuse. I can't imagine how difficult it is for someone to see God as a loving Father with such a terrible experience with their earthly father. But that is where the Spirit of God comes in, to heal and mend. I pray that all who have had an experience like this that causes struggle in their relationship with God would find that healing!

Lastly, we then have physical healing. This is what most people think of when we talk about healing. Jesus Christ has commissioned us to heal all manner of sickness.

> *"And these signs will follow those who believe: In My name they will cast out demons; they will speak with new tongues; they will take up serpents; and if they drink anything deadly, it will by no means hurt them; they will lay hands on the sick, and they will recover."*
>
> *Mark 16:17-18*

Healing the sick and casting out devils, these things should not be rare. Look at how often the disciples performed these same miracles after Jesus ascended. There is no reason we can't do them today. However, we must remember that the signs follow us; we should not chase after the signs.

> *"Is anyone among you sick? Let him call for the elders of the church and let them pray over him with oil in the name of the Lord."*
>
> *James 5:16*

The Blood of Christ deals with sin and salvation (Ephesians 1:7), the name of Christ deals with sickness (James 5:16), the Word of God deals with temptation (Matthew 4:1-11). We have been equipped for every challenge we face.

> *"But He was wounded for our transgressions, He was bruised for our iniquities; the chastisement for our peace was upon Him, and by His stripes we are healed."*
>
> *Isaiah 53:5*

This is the healing that Jesus performed in His life and ministry. A recent example happened last week, I came home from work, and one of our dog's eye was swollen nearly shut. The last time this had happened, our dog had cracked a tooth, and it cost several hundred in vet bills. We didn't have the money for it as finances were tight. My wife and I agreed in prayer. Within the hour, the swelling had gone down.

I do want to make a point about healing. Not all will be healed. There is a rising of bad theology that tells us God will always heal. That is His character, and if we look at the life of Christ, He healed all that He prayed for. There is an important distinction to be made here. Jesus was and is God. Some think that when Jesus took on flesh, He gave up his divinity. He did not. He was fully God and fully man. Being God, He could heal all. Jesus is our healing! Not everyone always got healed, though, even in the life of the apostles (1 Timothy 5:23; 2 Timothy 4:20).

We have the Spirit of God within us, and He administers healing at His will, not ours. We can have the healing power of God flow through us, but we are not the source of it. Jesus is the source. As previously mentioned, when Jesus said we would do "greater things," Jesus was referring to greater in reach, not greater in power; we take what He has given us to the whole world, Jesus has all authority, and with it, He commissions us to go and heal.

By the power of God and the unction of the Holy Spirit, you can be the vessel with which God uses to heal the sick!

Working of Miracles

A miracle is an extraordinary event taken as a sign of the supernatural God. I'll explain this by going back to creation; when God created everything, He did it in a two-step process:

1. He spoke everything into existence
2. He instructed everything on "how" to exist.

He said, "Let there be," and there was. But later, we see God giving instructions to reproduce, vegetation after its kind, animals after theirs, man after their kind. In the second step of creation, God programmed nature into things. Everything works according to its nature. Like Newton's law of inertia, "an object in motion remains in motion unless acted upon in an equal and opposite force." All things work to their nature unless something or someone intervenes. I want to define the difference between luck and miracles clearly.

1. Miracle - When God steps in and works against something's nature.
2. Luck - a possibility of a thing happening naturally, usually with only a small percentage in its favor.

When one becomes skilled at a thing, then they have a greater probability of making something happen despite its potentially low percentage. When something happens outside of God's intervention and outside of one's skill, it is what we call *luck*.

Now, before I get too deep into this, I want to clarify that the Bible does talk about what we call luck in the sense of "beginners luck." In the story of Ahab and his death (1 Kings 22), we see that while on the battlefield, "a *certain* man drew a bow at random, and struck the king of Israel between the joints of his armor" (verse 34).

In this passage of Scripture, the archer was not aiming for the king's weak spot, despite his skill. So when the Scripture says "at random" or "by chance," this is not giving credit to the archer's skill or God's intervention. There was just a low probability of this happening. And before we say, no, it was God intervening; God will not give the credit of the work of His hand to something as trivial as chance. We see the same thing happen to Ruth:

> *"Ruth happened to come into the field belonging to Boaz...".*
>
> *Ruth 2:3*

The word for "hap," or "happen" in Hebrew is "miqreh," which can translate as "befall," "chance," or in modern-day terms, "luck." This passage says, "It just happened that Ruth came to this particular field." She happened to be in the right place at the right time. Again, there is no mention of God intervening or man planning this out. As Christians, we have this mentality that there is no such thing as "luck." But there are several instances in the Scripture where we see something happening by luck or chance.

As far as "good luck charms," they don't have any power in them. It's a superstitious belief. But we do have an interesting point to relate to biblically.

There were a few forms of Hebrew throughout history. The earliest form was called "block Hebrew." It did not have any rounded letters. If you were to take each of the Hebrew letters in block form and stack them, one on top of the other, you would get the shape of the Star of David. You can find videos of this on YouTube.

Now, since the law of God was written in Hebrew, and the Hebrew alphabet formed the shape of the Star of David, it was symbolic of one who kept the Word or Law of God. Some referred to it as a good luck charm. David had this star placed on all the shields in his palace.

Again, no luck comes from this symbol; it's merely symbolic. Those who obeyed the Law and kept the covenant were blessed by God, having a hedge of protection around them. (For more on the blessing and the curse, read Deuteronomy 28).

Types of Miracles

1   Creative Miracles
We see this throughout the creation story. God spoke everything into existence. God's creativity hasn't stopped. I know we don't necessarily see the creative works of God today, but I think that has more to do with where we place our faith than anything. We have tremendous confidence in modern medicine, and we

tend to doubt God's willingness to create miracles in our life.

I think the greatest creative miracle we have today is the creation of people. Having children is proof that God is not done creating. And when we understand that the spirit of a man comes from God, it shows He is still the One in charge of Life!

2 Nature Miracles

We see this several times throughout Scripture. Jesus calmed the storm (Mark 4:35-41). Jesus' first miracle was turning water into wine, which is also a creative miracle (John 2:1-11), also when Jesus fed the 5,000 (Mark 6:30-43).

3 Miracles that Defy Nature

Jesus walked on water. This is not doable in the natural realm without a supernatural intervention from God. We also see the miracle with Elisha and the windows oil (2 Kings 4:1-7). Amid a famine, with no food or water, the widow fed Elisha with the last of her oil. However, she received a miracle, from that point until the famine ended, the jar of oil never ran out.

In my life, I have had a few miracles that have happened, which were witnessed by others. Things that left us standing there wondering, "How...?" One where a group of us were driving on a wet road in Seattle, and as we came around a corner, traffic was at a dead stop. At our speed, there was no way to stop in time to prevent a collision. In a split second, we were hydroplaning; I prayed, "Lord save us". We stopped immediately.

4 Life Giving Miracles

Raising the dead is the main miracle. It may be considered that procreation can fit here, but that is the creation of a new being.

Several miracles happened daily for the Israelites for the forty years they wandered the wilderness (Nehemiah 9:6-37). Here is a list of them:

1. God would appear as a pillar of cloud by day, leading the Israelites to where they were to go. The cloud would rest on the tabernacle every day they were to station themselves.
2. God would appear as a pillar of fire by night.
3. The Spirit of God would Instruct them on what to do daily.
4. Manna was provided from Heaven every morning until the sun came up and melted it.
5. God provided water from the rock every day to keep them hydrated in the wilderness
6. The clothes of the Israelites never wore out the whole 40 years they wandered the desert.
7. Their feet did not swell during the wandering in the wilderness.

Though there are different types of miracles, God gives them all to us, and we must be obedient to Him and work in faith to see them come about.

CHAPTER 10

TONGUES / DIVERSE LANGUAGES

The spiritual gift of speaking in tongues or diverse languages has to be one of the most confusing things concerning spiritual gifts. I specifically remember having this conversation growing up, why would God have us speak in tongues and then seek an interpretation for it? Why would He not just tell us what is on His mind?

In the 15 years I spent seeking out an understanding of the gifts, I knew there was something more about tongues. But it didn't seem like I would ever find the reason. And then I heard Perry Stone preach a message, "Not All Tongues are the Same." This was eye-opening to me. Over the next few years, I would seek to understand this further. So here is what I've learned, with some of my own experiences, an overview of the types of tongues;

1. Initially (the baptism of the Holy Spirit),
2. The Gift of Tongues,
3. Diverse Tongues

Initially (the Baptism of the Holy Spirit)
I believe that speaking in tongues initially is the spiritual equivalent of a driver's license. You wouldn't let someone operate your Rolls Royce without first proving their willingness to abide by the laws of the road. Likewise, God wants you to prove your submission to Him before He allows you to operate in the other gifts of the Spirit.

Initially, God wants me to submit my tongue to Him. If my most unruly member can submit entirely to God, then I can submit my whole body to the work of His Kingdom. And that's why Jesus commanded the disciples to wait till the gift of God had been given. Peter has just denied Jesus three times. But once the Holy Spirit empowered him, he submitted wholly to the power of God.

When we look at the account in the book of Acts, it never says that "speaking in tongues" is the sign that must accompany all who are filled or baptized in the Spirit. (Note: we say baptized because there is a difference between being filled with the Spirit upon salvation, as seen in John 20:2, and being empowered to do the works and ministry of God. When we become baptized, the Holy Spirit overflows from our life into those around us). Now three of the five accounts mention speaking in tongues directly and refer to the people "knowing" they received the Holy Spirit because they spoke in tongues.

1. Acts 2:1-4 (tongues),
2. Acts 8:14-19,
3. Acts 9:17-19,
4. Acts 10:44-46 (tongues),
5. Acts 19:1-7 (tongues)

In Acts 8, it says Simon saw that the Spirit was given. There was a sign of some kind; though it isn't detailed, it makes sense then that it would be the same sign in all the other instances. In Acts 10, we are told that the circumcised believers were astonished that the Gentiles would receive the Holy Spirit, and the evidence was that the Gentiles were "speaking in tongues."

So why is speaking in tongues the sign of the baptism of the Holy Spirit? In James, we are told that the tongue is the most complex member to gain control over, and the man who does is a "perfect man." We speak in tongues as a "surrendering" of our most stubborn member. If I can submit my tongue to God, I can submit everything. Since the purpose of the initial infilling of the Holy Spirit is to surrender to God, there is no need to have an interpretation. It isn't about God speaking to us but us surrendering to Him.

The Gift of Tongues

This is most often operated in the church. I think one of the reasons for the gift of speaking in tongues is to practice unity in the church. One speaks, and another interprets. The gift of tongues, when accompanied by the interpretation of tongues, serves the same purpose as prophecy - to edify the church (1 Corinthians 14:4-5).

> *"He who speaks in a tongue edifies himself, but he who prophesies edifies the church. I wish you all spoke with tongues, but even more that you prophesied; for he who prophesies is greater than he who speaks with tongues, unless indeed he interprets, that the church may receive edification."*

Though tongues accompanied with the interpretation does edify like prophecy, tongues do not always bring a prophetic word – though they can.

Let me give you an example, a few years ago, a minister named Ivan Tait laid his hands on me. He then began to pray for me in tongues. Then he interpreted the message in tongues, and it was a prophetic word. This was the first time I had ever had that happen to me, and this was the most beautiful experience of tongues and interpretation I had ever seen.

When we operate in the gift of tongues, it is not us speaking; God is speaking through His Spirit. And He speaks in His native tongue. Since we can't understand His language, it has to be interpreted. But we only need a verbal interpretation when spoken out in a public setting. This is because I can receive the interpretation in my head, but it doesn't benefit anyone who can't hear it. The gift of tongues are not only for a public setting but can also happen in your private prayer time. When this happens, you still need an Interpretation, but it doesn't need to be relayed verbally because you are the only one who needs to understand it.

Just like the high priest on the day of atonement, he would communicate to God directly in God's native language. The high priest had an understanding of God's language, and he could speak fluently during that time alone. Unlike the high priest, we don't know it and can't speak it fluently, so we must also ask Him to interpret it.

Diverse Tongues
This would include speaking in other languages of both men and angels:

> "Though I speak with the tongues of men and of angels...."
>
> *1 Corinthians 13:1*

124

Do we have to pray in tongues to pray in the Spirit? Many people teach that praying in the Spirit is exclusively in tongues, but that is untrue.

> *"...praying always with all prayer and supplication in the Spirit...."*
>
> *Ephesians 6:18*

All prayer in the Spirit. Again, the Bible talks about eleven types of prayer, such as the prayer of agreement, repentance, binding and loosing, thanksgiving, etc. So when I pray any of these types of prayer, I can do so in alignment with the Spirit of God. This does mean praying in tongues, but it also means every other prayer. This clarifies that we are to pray according to the will of God and not our own.

Tongues of Men
The purpose is often when one is among others with a different native language. If you were to speak to someone who only spoke German and you don't know German, then that is both a diverse tongue - you never learned it - and also a sign to the unbeliever (1 Corinthians 14:22).

There are ten main languages in the world: English, Spanish, Chinese, Russian, etc. There are over 1,600 known to be common and over 1,000 spoken among the lesser-known tribes throughout the world. God knows them all, and if He desires to, He can use us as a vessel to speak to those of any language directly, whether you know and understand the language or not. I know a woman who prays in Hebrew every time she prays in her prayer language.

Tongues of Angels

I heard a minister talk about this before. He was a missionary to Russia. And someone asked him a very unusual question, "When you are in Russia, are you tempted to sin in your native language (English) or Russian?" He didn't know right then. So upon returning to Russia, he realized that while there, he was tempted in their native tongue. And in America, he was tempted in English. Like people, not all angels or devils speak all languages; only God is omniscient.

There have been two times in my own life I have heard my prayer language change to a different language. I prayed against spiritual things I couldn't speak in my natural language. As we become more aware of the spiritual battle around us, it's easier to see the demonic activity. Sometimes we pray and rebuke those spirits in their native tongue, not ours.

Devotion

This would be praying in tongues to edify yourself. No two people have the same devotional prayer language. Because it is your spirit praying to God. So it will be different.

> *"But you dear friends, build yourself up in your most holy faith [by] praying in the Holy Spirit."*
>
> *Jude 1:20*

There is no better way to fight depression and emotional lows than to pray in the spirit. With each prayer we pray, there is an outcome. A prayer of repentance brings forgiveness. A prayer of agreement brings unity. Praying in the Holy Spirit brings edification!

Worship

"What is the conclusion *then? I will pray with the spirit, and I will also pray with the understanding. I will sing with the spirit, and I will also sing with the understanding".*

1 Corinthians 14:15

We can both pray and sing with our spirit. Praying with your spirit instead of your understanding is to bypass your mind. When we are tempted, we are tempted in our native language. Satan can't tempt me with the language of my spirit. So it is unhindered prayer. Another reason, if I'm praying for healing, it's easy for me to doubt what I pray. So when I pray in the spirit, I cannot doubt what I'm praying!

Intercessory

"Likewise the Spirit also helps in our weaknesses. For we do not know what we should pray for as we ought, but the Spirit Himself makes intercession for us with groanings which cannot be uttered".

Roman 8:26

This is the most intense prayer I have ever prayed. On two occasions, I have had a considerable burden from the Lord to pray for someone. I had no idea what was going on in their life. But I couldn't shake it. And for at least an hour, it was the most intense prayer that I couldn't even speak. Then, instantly, the burden lifted. Just like that, it was gone.

The Interpretation of Tongues

Regarding interpreting the gift of tongues, remember it is an interpretation, not a translation. I may interpret it as, "thus saith the Lord..." and you may interpret it as "the Lord would say to you...". Being an interpretation, it may vary. You may have an interpretation as you're speaking in tongues, and upon finishing, someone else may interpret it publicly. Every time I've known this to happen, even though the word choice may vary, the message doesn't.

When interpreting a prayer language, I have found when I intercede for someone, it's a bit more vague. I can't always interpret it word for word; that is, I don't always know the extent of what I'm praying, and I don't need to. But I can understand for whom and what I pray. God will usually give me a picture in my mind's eye about what I'm praying for. God directs my thoughts. Have you ever been going about your business during the day? Suddenly, you have a thought. Maybe a revelation? Perhaps a Scripture verse, or you think of someone you haven't seen or heard of in a while? God is drawing your attention to that. And He does that when we pray in the Spirit. And while praying for someone or a situation, my thoughts may change suddenly. This isn't a distraction, but God shows me what I am praying for. There are times when someone needs prayer at that moment, and God calls upon His people to intercede. Thus it is essential to "watch and pray." Always be prepared to be God's voice on the earth. Always be submissive to His Spirit and His will.

CHAPTER 11

PROPHECY

There are three sources for a prophetic word. First, God will reveal the prophetic to us by His Spirit (2 Peter 1:21). Second, false prophets, who get their prophecy from evil spirits (1 John 4:1). Third is the prophecy from man's own heart (Jeremiah 23:16,24-25).

One thing that is common in services where the prophetic is active is that the one giving the prophecy tends to ask a lot of questions before speaking the word forth. When someone comes and prophesies over me, and they start asking me questions, I have a question that arises in me, "who are you hearing from"? "Why do you need to know so much about me before telling me what God has to say"? Because God doesn't need to ask me questions before He tells me what He will do in my life. God already knows that I'm married, where I work, what I worry about, and the list goes on.

Prophet of God

> "Let two or three prophets speak, and let the others judge."
>
> 1 Corinthians 14:29

If you claim to have a prophetic word but avoid accountability, then you are not a prophet. When a prophetic word comes forth, the others must judge it. Does it align with the Word of God? Is it confirming? Or is it just vague mumbo jumbo?

There are some churches you go to where everyone has a prophetic word; that's when you know people are getting in the flesh, as we are told, two or three at the most. Continuing in 1 Corinthians 14:30-32

> *"For you can all prophesy one by one, that all may learn and all may be encouraged. And the spirits of the prophets are subject to the prophets. For God is not* the author *of confusion but of peace, as in all the churches of the saints".*

There is order to how God speaks. He doesn't interrupt Himself. If the pastor is preaching the sermon, there will not be a prophetic word or message in tongues because God is speaking through the pastor by the Word.

The prophecy must be delivered in an orderly fashion. If more than three prophesy, or they begin interrupting each other, it isn't of God. "Well, I can't help it; when God gives me a Word, as Jeremiah said, there is a fire in my bones. I can't help but speak". No, Paul tells us that the spirit of the prophet is subject to the prophet. So yes, you can hold your tongue. You can wait until it is an appropriate time.

> *"If anyone thinks himself to be a prophet or spiritual, let him acknowledge that the things which I write to you are the commandments of the Lord." 1 Corinthians 14:37*

What Paul is saying here is that no office of ministry and no individual working in the gifts is above the written Word of God. This is how the prophet is to be judged. He says if he is ignorant, let him be ignorant. Some people won't learn. They have rules that they believe trump all else, including God's. With all this being said;

> *"Therefore, brethren, desire earnestly to prophesy, and do not forbid to speak with tongues. Let all things be done decently and in order."*
>
> *1 Corinthians 14:39-40*

I have heard the gift of prophecy described many times - not for what it is but - for how it should be delivered. Check this out in 1 Corinthians 14:3:

> *"But the one who prophesies speaks to people for their edification, exhortation and comfort."*

And with that, it is often taught that prophecy is not a "foretelling of future events" but a means to encourage people. That is a service gift which is separate from prophecy. Here is the definition of the word prophecy as used in 1 Corinthians 12-14:

> *"A disclosure emulating from divine inspiration and declaring the purposes of God, whether by reproving and admonishing the wicked, or by comforting the afflicted, or revealing things hidden esp. by foretelling future events."*

Prophecy is, by definition, a foretelling of future events. Paul clarifies here that the prophesy, so long as it is from God, will be brought in a manner that edifies, exhorts, and comforts. This does not mean that all prophecy is "only good". The promise that is associated with the prophetic is a good result, but the condition of our obedience must be met to find that promise.

Look at the book of Revelation for that. God is pouring out His wrath on those who reject Him. And after many judgements, we are told that "they repented not". God's desire is for all in this tribulation period to repent and be saved. It is their rebellion that fills His wrath to overflowing.

Under the unction of the Holy Spirit, anyone can prophesy. You may be struggling with an addiction or sin, but God can and does use broken vessels. But operating in the gift of prophecy does not require the level of devotion that the office of the prophet does. There is a need for complete dedication in your life to operate in the office, not so with the gift. Because of this reason, many prophesy amiss. And I say that because I don't believe people always intend to misguide people, they want to be used by God. This is one gift we are encouraged to seek (1 Corinthians 14:1), and it's easy amid our zeal to speak out of emotion and not on God's Word.

How does prophecy work? As we saw in John 16, the Spirit hears the word of the Lord and relays it to us. We hear the word from the Spirit and relay that message. Prophecy, in my own experience, is rarely a quote of "thus saith the Lord." That is how it worked for Jeremiah, but usually, it's just us speaking the message from God.

If I'm at work and my boss tells Ryan, "Find Philip and have him clean the third floor." Ryan then finds me and says, "Hey, Dustin wants you to go to the third floor and clean." Ryan didn't quote Dustin, but he still relayed the message accurately. That, more often than not, is how prophecy works.

False Prophets

If a prophet teaches that one can manifest things by speaking them forth and that God will honor that, then this so-called prophet is mixing the sacred with the secular.

> *"And we heard this voice which came from heaven when we were with Him on the holy mountain. And so we have the prophetic word confirmed, which you do well to heed as a light that shines in a dark place, until the day dawns and the morning star rises in your hearts; knowing this first, that no prophecy of Scripture is of any private interpretation, for prophecy never came by the will of man, but holy men of God spoke* as they were *moved by the Holy Spirit."*
>
> *2 Peter 1:16-21*

We are warned that false prophets will enter the church and mislead people. This isn't a possibility but a fact. Jesus said it would happen, so we must be aware of this. We judge the prophecy, but we also must discern the spirit, whether it is of God, man, or Satan.

Prophet of Man

Third, and I believe that this one is what we need to be aware of now more than ever. People can prophesy from their own heart (Jeremiah 23:16,24-25); they prophesy lies in the name of God. They are speaking out of the desires of their own heart. Some are doing this sincerely, not wanting to mislead people; this is where church leadership must step in and correct the error.

We must never give way to this kind of behavior. God isn't wrong. However, people often are. If you are unsure whether you are hearing from God or not, don't speak. Again, God will not speak a word to you today that contradicts His written Word.

A Good Word

It's common among many today to prophesy "good things are coming your way," and they leave it at that.

> *"For all the promises of God in Him are Yes, and in Him Amen, to the glory of God through us."*
>
> *2 Corinthians 1:20*

We have been given the best gift beyond what we could have ever hoped for, the blood of Christ. That is free and brings us salvation, eternally, with our Lord. That doesn't mean it's all a walk in the park. When we become saved, we enter into a battle over our souls. No one in a war cries, "He hurt me! Stop it!" You have to fight.

> *"For you have need of endurance, so that after you have done the will of God, you may receive the promise."*
>
> *Hebrews 10:36*

We must persist in the good fight. Persistence doesn't begin when you become saved. It starts when things get tough. When you want to quit, then persistence kicks in. If we endure, we will see the promise. We must be obedient to the Word and will of God to receive His promise.

His promises for you are conditional; you must remain in Him! God will reward us for our faithfulness, and sometimes He gives us a glimpse of what is in store so that we remain. It's not just good for you and only ever good. Don't be deceived if someone claims you will be blessed and find no struggle ahead. If there is no struggle, then take caution because we are to fight the good fight (1 Timothy 6:12). I'm not saying there won't be seasons of rest in our life. God does do that for us. But to teach that every prophetic word from God will be positive is just unbiblical. Throughout Scripture, the Old and New Testaments often warned of judgment if the people did not repent. Not every time, but a lot of the time.

God's Purpose

Have you wondered what God's purpose is in your life? He wants us to surrender to Him and glorify Him. We must keep in mind that there is a difference between God's perfect plan and God's purpose.

> *"And do not be conformed to this world, but be transformed by the renewing of your mind, that you may prove what is that good and acceptable and perfect will of God."*
>
> *Romans 12:2*

Good as opposed to bad. Acceptable is pleasing. Perfect meaning, nothing better. You can be in God's purpose but not in his perfect will. His perfect will is for you to remain sinless. God will always be able to use you for his purpose no matter where you are. However, that doesn't mean you are always in His perfect plan. But that's the great thing about His saving grace, the blood of Jesus covers our sins! He continually calls us to Him. I don't believe God is upset by our failures or when we stumble and fall. So long as we get back up and continue to pursue Him. God can't be surprised by our failures; He already knows all of our sins, and He loves us anyway. We must ensure we don't use this as an excuse to remain in sin; we must remain in Him (John 15).

We live in a culture that has an entitlement mentality. "I deserve stuff, I should not be asked to work for it". It's so easy to sit there and complain about your situation. God will help you out of any struggle, sin, or battle, but don't ask for the result before you take the first step. He will not give you the second step until you fulfill the first! Get up off your ashes of self-loathing. God will not call you without empowering you to meet the call!

Warring with the Prophetic

> *"This charge I entrust to you Timothy my child, in accordance with the prophecies previously made about you that by them you may wage a good warfare".*
>
> *1 Timothy 1:18*

The personal prophecies given to an individual are spiritual weapons to use in warfare. Satan likes to raise doubt about God's call on our life. It is vital that we hold on to all God says to us. Satan will attempt to discourage us concerning the anointing/call that God has given us. That is when we must lean on the prophetic promises God gives us.

I think it is important to write down what God speaks to us. God only speaks truth over us and to us. Satan speaks lies. So we can use the Word of God to war against the enemy.

In the same way, as soon as we receive a prophetic promise from God, it will put a target on our backs. Satan is now out to get us. He wishes to stop us from fulfilling it. He will do it by any means necessary. He will speak negatively to us, trying to arouse feelings of doubt, discouragement, and depression.

Hold on to the promise of God. We are to war with the prophetic!

CHAPTER 12

LOVING GOD

What is the purpose of these gifts without salvation? What good is it to heal the sick physically only for them to die lost? What is the point in deliverance from devils if that same person dies and goes to hell? (David Diga Hernandez, 2023)

It is by no chance that the chapter on love, which has been the topic of many sermons and Bible studies, is sandwiched between the two chapters about the gifts of the Spirit. God's compassion extends beyond those who have chosen Him. God heals and delivers His children because of His covenant; he heals and delivers sinners because of His mercy. God does not have mercy for the physical need without mercy for the spiritual need. The purpose of the gifts are, number one, to point people to the blood of Jesus for salvation, and number two, a means for God to minister to us. The focus in some churches is the gifts of the Spirit. It is so stressed that we have access to these gifts and we can walk in them that we forget the primary purpose, leading people to Christ and making Jesus famous!

I like how Melissa Daugherty says it, If you never got a miracle in your life, would you be okay with that? If you never received a prophetic word or a healing, would you still love God just as much? Is Jesus enough? (Melissa Daugherty, 2023). I can't tell you why so many people experience lifelong illnesses when they are faithful servants of the Lord, but I know they do. Do not base your salvation on what God can do for you; base your salvation on loving God! The moment you shift your focus from Who Jesus is to what He does, you are in danger!

What does loving God mean to you? I have realized that loving God doesn't mean the same thing to me today as it did last year. Sometimes I'm so dedicated to loving Him; others, not so much. Sometimes loving God is seen in my desire to leave my life of sin and pursue Him wholeheartedly. Other times it's enough not to lash out at my coworkers, and even in those times, I still find myself failing. I'm so glad that the blood of Christ is not based on my emotions. My salvation is steady and true no matter how I feel or what I'm going through. But I think it is important to realize that we are either growing daily or dying gradually.

It is a great practice to ask God daily to help you love Him more and more. Become aware of the presence of God every day. Give Him time to impress Himself on you today. Then when you get up tomorrow, do the same!

A Future Wedding

As the bride of Christ, we have a role to prepare for the big day. When Jesus said in John that He goes to His Father's house to prepare a place for us, that is not a cue for us to sit back and wait. He is coming back for a bride without spot or wrinkle. He is preparing a place; we must prepare ourselves. It was common among Jewish men to shower their brides with gifts before their wedding. We see this with Isaac and Rebekah. Here is something to keep in mind:

1. Israel is considered the wife of God (Isaiah 54:5-8; Ezekiel 16:8-21)
2. The church is the bride of Christ (Ephesians 5:22-33).

In Genesis 24, we see a picture of God's plan of salvation for all humanity summed up into a single narrative. Abraham is sending his servant Eliezer to find a wife for his son.

While he was doing so, Eliezer had 10 of his master's camels loaded with gifts for the future bride of the son. Eliezer goes to a well outside the city when the women come to draw water. While he waits, he cries out to God. This is the first time the Scripture speaks of prayer in the traditional sense of today. He proceeds in his prayer to ask for a sign, not only will the right woman draw water for Eliezer, but also for his ten camels. Camels drink as little as 10-15 gallons of water up to 30 gallons at a time. That is potentially 300 gallons of water she will be drawing for a stranger. This is the evening, and everyone is getting ready to go in for the night and sleep.

Rebekah shows up, being very attractive, and with a servant's heart, she does more than anyone expects. Rebekah was chosen in part because of her concern for others and her warm love. Beautiful though she was, that was considered secondary. Let's look at how this story relates to the gifts Jesus showers His bride with before His return for the wedding;

1. Abraham is symbolic of God the Father

2. Eliezer (senior servant) plays the role of the Holy Spirit
3. Isaac is symbolic of Jesus as the groom soon to be wed.
4. Rebekah would be the Bride of Christ/church
5. Eliezer came riding on one of the nine camels and had nine loaded with gifts – The nine gifts of the Spirit (*1 Corinthians 12*) and the nine fruit of the Spirit (*Galatians 5:22-23*).
6. The act of drawing water is what the church does when pulling on the Spirit of God.
7. Nose Ring/Two bracelets are engagement rings. The nose ring and jewels were usually 1 to 1.5 inches in diameter and traditionally strung on the right nostril.

Christ's first coming was to find Himself a bride. Upon leaving, the Servant/Holy Spirit showered the bride with gifts. These gifts are a means to prepare us for the coming wedding day. As previously mentioned, we won't need healing in Heaven; we won't get sick. We won't need faith in Heaven; we will see God face to face! These gifts are just a taste of what's to come for the believer. We are in part now; we will be whole then!

There will be a marriage supper of the Lamb (Jesus Christ) in the future (Revelation 19:9). This is where the church, the bride of Christ, will present herself. We get to partake in this. So like every bride before her wedding, we are to prepare ourselves.

"Husbands, love your wives, just as Christ also loved the church and gave Himself for her, that He might sanctify

*and cleanse her with the washing of
water by the word, that He might
present her to Himself a glorious
church, not having spot or wrinkle or
any such thing, but that she should be
holy and without blemish."*

Ephesians 5:25-27

Without spot or wrinkle. Sinless! Holy! This is
what Christ is looking for in His bride. And the Holy
Spirit is here to empower us to follow in His steps and
be Christ-like.

Not a loving God

Love is central to any properly nourished relationship,
especially between a groom and his bride. But we need
to have a clear understanding of what love is. I think we
as people tend to have a difficult time understanding the
character and nature of God. We look at God with our
limited understanding and question some of what He
does; how can He allow such evil in the world? How can
a loving God send people to Hell? The problem most
often comes from the way we question Him, "how can a
loving God?" God is not a loving God. He is not a being
that is capable of loving. We are loving people, but God
is not.

*"Beloved, let us love one another, for
love is of God; and everyone who loves
is born of God and knows God. He who
does not love does not know God, for
God is love."*

1 John 4:7-8

God *is* Love. With that in mind, we can find
correction in our mindset. Everything God does

expresses love, even what we don't consider love. Let's look at Exodus 15:3:

> "The LORD is a man of war; The LORD is His name."

Or Exodus 34:14:

> "...For the Lord, Whose name is Jealous, is a jealous God."

Our God, Who is love, is a God of war? He is a jealous God? Jealous is a title used in Scripture exclusively for God. It is a focus on His desire for an exclusive relationship. Remember, God is married to Israel (Ezekiel 16:8-21), and no husband wants to share his wife with another man. John Parsons from Hebrew for Christians says it best:

> "Jealousy is when the fear of losing love evokes a healthy zeal to protect oneself against loss."

It is ok to be defensive over the things you love. Not being defensive is a sign that you don't have a love for it, "Love always protects" (1 Corinthians 13:7).

A fun thing to do is to go through Scripture and replace the name of God with Love. It may help you better grasp that all He does is love.

Seven Types of Love
Love is not an emotion; Love extends beyond that; it's eternal, it's powerful, and it can't be stopped. We can see Love in so many different ways in our lives, and some of those might not be the way we expect. I did a study years ago on Love. I found that there are seven types of Love we can experience in life.

1. Ahab - love like a friend. This was Abraham's name.
2. Ah'ba - Familial love. Romantic, covenant, loyalty.
3. Ha'saq - to set one's affection toward, a desire, attach to or to bind like a kindred spirit - David and Jonathan had this kind of love.
4. Ra'ham - to have compassion on, show mercy toward, to take pity on. This is derived from the word "rah'mim," meaning "mercy" or "compassion."
5. Dod - as an uncle, cousin, relative, beloved one. This can range from friendship to romance.
6. Ra'ya - darling, beloved. Formally: companion. The woman is the object of a man's love (marriage).
7. Ga'bim - devotion, love, much love, very lovely. As to a teacher or a rabbi.

God/Love should permeate our lives and into the lives of those around us. There should be evidence in our life of God in all we do, and everywhere we go. Like Moses, when he met with God, he needed to cover his face with a veil so the glory of God would not blind the people.

The Mystery of Strange Fire

There have been times in my life when I have experienced the presence of God in such a powerful way. And then I move on. I tend to live off of that high for a while; like it's been said, there "ain't no high like the Most High!" I've found that I often like to recreate the same move of God. Now, a lot of meeting with God and encountering Him has to do with the atmosphere. We have to remove distractions and enter with an attitude of reverence and worship; this is what God desires of us.

> *"For where two or three are gathered together in My name, I am there in the midst of them."*
>
> *Matthew 18:20*

It's the same picture we have in Heaven. When Isaiah was before the throne of God, He was surrounded by the angels who were worshipping Him (Isaiah 6). He inhabits the praise of His people (Psalm 22:3).

God will move as He wills in whatever manner He sees fit. There is a danger in becoming ritualistic in our worship of Him. We see this with the two sons of Aaron, the high priest. Upon looking at the story, you'll notice it starts with a look at genealogies. For many of us, we overlook them, they're boring, filled with names of people we can't pronounce, and it doesn't impact our life, right? There are a lot of things that are hidden here.

In Numbers 3:1-4 we see the generations of who we are told are Aaron and Moses. But Moses' descendants aren't mentioned here, only Aaron's. This is because Moses taught the Torah to them. Now Moses taught the Torah to everyone. But Aaron's sons, Nadab and Abihu, really took a likening to Moses. And it's thought that when one teaches Torah to another, they become a father to them. We talk of having spiritual fathers in our life, and that is what Moses was to these two boys. I think this is something we all do. We idolize the life and teaching of someone and try to mimic that. It's something that a lot of us are very easily capable of if we are not careful. We idolize the teachings of others and even look at their relationship with God wanting it for ourselves. But instead of seeking God on His terms, we do it the way we see others doing it.

It is much like Peter, who saw Jesus walking on the water. Jesus gave Peter the same command He gave the rest of the disciples, "Get in the boat and go to the other side." Peter was okay with this command until he saw another way, walking on water. So what did Peter do? He didn't step out in faith as many teach. I believe Peter stepped out in rebellion. He bargained with Jesus, "Are you sure you put me in the right place? I think I could do pretty good over there with You".

He saw a different way, a more praiseworthy way, and instead of going through the same thing Jesus did, which was to pray all night, he thought that he could step into that ministry, so to speak, and do what God hadn't called him to do. He slept all night and wanted the same results as the One who had prayed all night.

How often do we do that in our own life? We have an idea, and we think we would serve God so well in that area, so we chase it. In so doing, we step out of God's anointing and favor, and we fail. And maybe what we desire is precisely what God is calling us to do, but we go about it incorrectly; we don't spend enough time preparing.

We are then told that Nadab and Abihu brought "strange fire" before the Lord, and because of it, they were killed. However, we aren't told directly why they were killed. What made this fire strange? Listen closely to how they died, as there are a lot of similarities to what happened with Moses on the mountain. In Exodus 19, we see that fire and cloud came down on the mountain, and Moses went up. He had the Tablets containing the ten commandments. Later, when the Tabernacle was finished, Aaron's two sons immediately ran to it with fire and smoke before the altar of God, which contained the Ten Commandments. They wanted the experience that Moses had! This was another Mount Sinai experience. The difference is that they weren't commanded to do this; they wanted to do this. The name Nadab comes from the word Nadiv which means "volunteer." They wanted so much to commune with the divine that it was almost as if they were trying to summon God.

This is okay to want to draw near to God. But in those instances, we must ensure we approach God correctly. God instructed them on how to do this. They could enter as the high priest once a year, but they didn't want to wait.

It is a blessing to find a great teacher. I had one years ago; I would hang on to every word he said. This was a man who knew God. I wanted to learn everything I could from this man. And it's important to have a teacher greater than yourself. The danger is that you can lose your identity to that. You can make your life about becoming like them and not like the One they follow.

As you seek more of God, I pray you aren't led astray by the life of others. I pray you will find God and follow after Him, heart and soul. Learn to hear His voice; learn to follow Him. As Paul said in 1 Corinthians 11:1, "Follow me as I follow Christ." May we not lose sight of the One Who called us.

Slain in the Spirit

There are forms of strange fire today. There are ways we try to summon God because of what we have seen of others. There are times when strange things happen in services when the Spirit of God is moving.

Let me give an example from my own life. When I was growing up in church, there was rarely a tangible display of the manifestation of God through the gifts. One time I remember we had a youth group come over to help us do a week-long outreach. Before we went out one day, we were praying, and I remember having this girl pray for me. She was a butch. I'm not being mean, but she was big-boned and intimidating. She came to me and placed her hand on my head. While praying, she was pushing me, so naturally, I was stepping back. Two others came behind me and prevented me from moving back further. She then told me not to resist the Holy Spirit and to give in to Him. I was baffled. Ultimately, she pushed me back, and the others laid me down on the ground. They then proceeded to move to the next person.

I remember the whole time while on the ground thinking, "What just happened?" I was confused and freaked while looking around to see what everyone else was doing. I was uncomfortable and wanted to get up. I'm thinking, "What kind of ungodly thing are they doing?" I seriously thought to myself that this was some occult practice. I was scared that if my family found out, they would rebuke me. I wasn't slain in the spirit; I was pushed by the flesh.

I have since come to realize that when we have an encounter with God, we do sometimes have a physical reaction. I understand how people can't stand in the presence of God. We see examples in Scripture; look at Saul on the road to Damascus (Acts 22). This, however, was not the Spirit Who laid me out; it was the youth praying for me.

Then we also see people emotionally wrecked. I find some similarities between the emotional reaction when we see a husband reunited with his wife after his return from war. We get emotional with encounters. I am convinced that both of these can be legit works of God. However, there are those who, for whatever reason, have responses that aren't consistent with the character and nature of God. Though I have never personally witnessed some of these behaviors, I know of people who have, seeing people running around acting like chickens. If God wanted you to act like a chicken, He would have created you as a chicken. I'm not saying that this behavior is sinful, but I do wonder how genuine this is. God is not a God of disorder but of peace. We have been created as intelligent beings, and our worship of Him should reflect that. Anything less than that is insulting.

People respond differently when encountering a holy God; don't misunderstand me. But we need to have discretion. At what point do people step outside the natural behavior of one who has experienced God and get into the flesh? This is where the "discerning of spirits" would be in operation.

And the responsibility for this falls to church leadership. We need to teach people what is acceptable and what is not. I mean no disrespect, but I have an example here. Some people have a borderline personality disorder, where they, at times, act out emotionally in ways that don't fit a particular situation. And I think that at times amid the work of God, people step out of a worshipful attitude and into fleshly actions.

I knew a girl who, years ago, gave a testimony of her time at a Christian college. They were learning how to move in the Spirit. And like I've said, this is ok. We need to teach people what is acceptable behavior and to discern the Spirit of God from the human spirit. But she said sometimes it is acceptable to "fake it until you make it." You cannot fake a move of God. He doesn't honor cheap imitations. Seek God and allow Him to give you an authentic experience. Don't pretend and justify yourself by saying, "God will honor this. He will see my desire, and in time I'll experience Him". Some people feel that your faith isn't genuine unless you have some supernatural encounter with God every few weeks. Don't let that attitude take over. Because the moment you do and don't experience Him, you begin to doubt your faith.

If you desire a real encounter with God, spend more time in the Word of God and pray.

Conclusion

We must remember that, above all else, it's not about us. The gifts are about God's Love *for* us expressed *to* us. We must never lose sight of God!

There was a Valentine's Day commercial years ago that said, "Valentine's Day is not about celebrating me, and it's not about celebrating you; it's about celebrating us." The gifts come from God to remind us of His love for us. We celebrate having access. He celebrates the joy we receive. They are a means for us to introduce God's blessings. When we rejoice in the gift and neglect the giver the gift loses its value. And as we do this, the relationship we should develop gets pushed to the wayside. We cannot allow ourselves to lose sight of God while enjoying His blessings for us. They are a means for us and God to mutually celebrate our relationship. Anyone can have access to them. But again, they are a byproduct of our relationship with Him. Submit to Him. Draw near to God, and He shall draw near to you!

As I have previously mentioned, I grew up in a Pentecostal church, though there wasn't much teaching on the gifts of the Spirit, none that I recall anyway. I had a lot of questions that I don't feel were ever answered.

I knew that being baptized in the Spirit and speaking in tongues was the next step in my journey, and, while I was at camp, I was maybe 12, and I received just that. At an altar call the very first night, I went up to pray. In these kinds of church meetings, there is usually an altar call dedicated to receiving the baptism of the Spirit. This was not one of those times. I wasn't up there for that. I remember thinking, "God, I don't know or care how you do this; I just want more of You."

Like Acts describes what appeared to be tongues of fire, I had a similar experience. Nothing was visible, but I immediately felt like my whole head was on fire, there was no pain but intense heat, and I just opened my mouth to speak. What came out wasn't English. I was speaking in a language I didn't know. Later I came to learn it was the language of God.

It was after that camp meeting that I felt like I had arrived. There was nothing else to gain in my walk with God. I had peaked in spirituality. I hadn't, but I thought I did.

Years later, I realized that this gift of praying in tongues was meant for me every day. I could worship God in a new way. But I didn't know that.

I have since met people who pray to receive the baptism, and after years they still haven't. I think part of the reason is because of ego. We become so concerned about what we say, how we may sound that we subconsciously hold on to the proverbial reigns. Another reason can be our desires. I like how David Diga Hernandez say, "Our overwhelming desire for an encounter with God can keep us from encountering God." We can get too caught up in ensuring everything is correct. Do I listen to worship music or not? Do I sing or sit in silence? Our emotions are one of the biggest hindrances to the work of God in our life. We don't feel like praying, so we don't. We get discouraged about our situations, so we allow things to distract us. For anyone seeking this, you must relinquish your right to yourself. Forget about forcing it; pray that God would speak through you and open your mouth.

It may sound odd. Everyone has their own prayer language, and we all have our accents, just like we do in any language. So we won't sound like the person next to us. And that's ok! Like a child learning to speak, much of what they say is noise. They have to learn to talk. Over time you will see your prayer language flourish.

Soul Winning for Jesus

> *"But you shall receive power when the Holy Spirit has come upon you; and you shall be witnesses to Me in Jerusalem, and in all Judea and Samaria, and to the end of the earth."*
>
> *Acts 1:8.*

If you want to have a better understanding of God, you have to befriend the Holy Spirit. He wants to be your friend. Next to the blood of Christ, a relationship with the Holy Spirit is the most important thing in your life. He is the most active in our lives but often the most neglected. When God speaks to us, it's by His Spirit. When He heals and delivers us, it is through the power of the Holy Spirit. You cannot find intimacy with God without understanding that truth.

The purpose of the outpouring of God's Spirit is to empower us to seek and save the lost. That must be the number one goal of any believer. If you love God, seek the lost! If you believe Jesus died for your salvation, share that with the lost! If you have the Spirit of God living in you, you must introduce Him to others.

It is okay to live and thrive and be successful on earth. It is okay to plan for your future, spend money on vacation and drive a nice car. But never forget the sacrifice of Jesus for the lost. You are commissioned to find the lost and testify about Jesus! When you encounter God, He overwhelms you with a fire for the lost! Don't let that fire fade.

A Prayer of Salvation
One must first be a child of God to receive the gifts of God. Many have taught a prayer we call "the sinner's prayer." A prayer where we ask Jesus into our hearts. Some say it's wrong because Jesus doesn't live in us; He is at the right hand of God. This is true. It is the Spirit of God Who dwells in us. But the fact that we confess Christ and believe in His redemptive work is what brings us salvation:

> *"that if you confess with your mouth the Lord Jesus and believe in your heart that God has raised Him from the dead, you will be saved. For with the heart one believes unto righteousness, and with the mouth confession is made unto salvation. For the Scripture says,* "Whoever believes on Him will not be put to shame."
>
> Romans 10:9-11

It's simple, if you believe the message of the cross, that we are all sinners (Romans 3:23), Christ, the Son of the Living God, came to die in our place (2 Corinthians 5:21), and you want Him to be Lord over your life, then confess with your mouth.

Jesus, I believe! Be Lord of my life!

Something that was common in church growing up and still is to this day, during the alter call at the end of the service, we are instructed, "Everyone close your eyes and bow your head. If you want to be saved, then repeat after me..." . The problem is we are making a group of *undercover* Christians who don't feel a need to do anything beyond saying a prayer. Jesus didn't die in secret; we shouldn't live for Him in secret!

> *"Therefore whoever confesses Me before men, him I will also confess before My Father who is in heaven. But whoever denies Me before men, him I will also deny before My Father who is in heaven."*

> *Matthew 10:32*

That is a command; there is no such thing as an undercover Christian. When we give our life to Christ, we enter into a war! A war with Satan over our eternity. No one can win a war alone. You have to surround yourself with other warriors. Instead of secretly praying, we must publicly rejoice with our newly saved brothers and sisters!

Once we have done this, you can access all God has for you. It's time to pray for the Spirit of God to live in you and overflow out of you!

Find a place where you are comfortable, maybe in your home, with no distractions, and worship God for a moment. A good piece of advice I received was that when you don't feel like praying, worship God. It is the Spirit of God who draws us to pray (John 14:6). Then pray to God, "Lord, I believe that You have saved me and that You have given gifts to me. I want to take hold of these gifts; I want to walk in the Spirit! I yield myself to You; I yield my tongue to You. May Your Spirit speak through me!" Just open your mouth and speak. Don't think. You are not trying to form sentences. You are allowing the Spirit of God to do that for you, through you!

155

I want to tell you a story I heard a while ago. I can't say where this story originated, but it is so relevant to this. A father was teaching his little girl to pray. And every night he would go into her room at bed and pray with her. After a few nights he told her that he wanted her to pray herself. To learn to talk to God. So he stepped outside her room and waited, listening. What he heard was baffling to him. She was singing her ABC's. This went on a few nights and he eventually came in after her song one night to ask her why she was singing her ABC's and not praying. She replied, "I'm just giving God all the letters and letting Him make the words".

This is praying in tongues!

Now that you have down the, it's time to find a Spirit-filled church to help you on our journey! Nothing is more excellent than having the Holy Spirit live with and in you. It is the most precious thing to walk with God, filled with His Spirit! May your journey begin here and flourish! I pray He would flow out of you into the lives of those around you!

Now may the Lord bless you and keep you, may the Lord make His face to shine upon you and be gracious to you. The Lord lift up His countenance upon you and give you peace!

Numbers 6:24-26

To the glory of God!

About the Author

Philip Reed is a writer/author who has studied at Berian: School of the Bible. He has served in several pastoral positions throughout the years and has a passion for preaching and writing. He and his wife enjoy theme parks and traveling. They have been married for eight years and live happily in Evansville IN.

www.TheHeartofGodbooks .com

Acknowledgments

To those who gave financially in
support of this endeavor

Miranda Reed
Patricia LaFollette
Andrew Tieken
Michael Speicher
Dustin Morris
Vicki Loehr
Chris White Tucker

Thank You!

Made in the USA
Middletown, DE
11 September 2024

60152424R00093